To Mary
with thanks
for your support
of my work.
Cynthia Jabrock

BEAUTIFUL BARRIER-FREE

A Visual Guide to Accessibility

BEAUTIFUL BARRIER-FREE

A Visual Guide to Accessibility

Cynthia Leibrock

with Susan Behar

VAN NOSTRAND REINHOLD
New York

To my husband, mother, father, brother, and our Christian faith, which inspired this book.

Library of Congress Catalog Card Number 91-47172
ISBN 0-442-00882-1

I(T)P Van Nostrand Reinhhold is a division of International Thomson
Publishing. ITP logo is a trademark under license.

Printed in Hong Kong.

Van Nostrand Reinhold
115 Fifth Avenue
New York, NY 10003

International Thomson Publishing
Berkshire House
168-173 High Holborn
London WC1V 7AA, England

Thomas Nelson Australia
102 Dodds Street
South Melbourne 3205
Victoria, Australia

Nelson Canada
1120 Birchmount Road
Scarborough, Ontario
M1K 5G4, Canada

16 15 14 13 12 11 10 9 8 7 6 5 4 3 2

Library of Congress Cataloging-in-Publication Data

Leibrock, Cynthia.
Beautiful barrier-free : a visual guide to accessibility / Cynthia
Leibrock ; with Susan Behar.
p.   cm.
Includes index.
ISBN 0-442-00882-1
1. Architecture and the handicapped—United States. I. Behar,
Susan. II. Title.
NA2545.A1L45   1992
720'.42'0973—dc20
91-47172
CIP

Contents

Foreword

On behalf of the 43 million Americans with disabilities, I applaud the dedication and understanding needed to produce this most valuable book. It contains a myriad of suggestions for making the world more accessible to those of us with limitations. And yet, the author's premise is that accommodations do not have to be ugly, noticeable, or expensive. Rather, some accommodations can be made easily and require only understanding and consideration of the impact of some disabilities to achieve a friendly barrier-free environment.

This book gives helpful hints for and demonstrates the range of needs of persons with disabilities—from ramps and elevators to simple furnishings and small adaptive equipment.

I hope that anyone who is designing or renovating space, or who has a family member with a disability will read this book. Our world will be a better place because we will be in there together, not separated by artificial and thoughtless barriers.

The world can be a beautiful place—for all of us.

James S. Brady
Vice Chairman, National Organization for Disabilities
Vice Chairman, National Head Injury Foundation

Preface

We all have physical and mental differences. Many of us have difficulty living independently and are handicapped by problems created not by our differences in ability or age, but by obstacles in buildings. The decisions of designers and architects can either disable us or offer us a different way of using the space, a way that provides freedom without the "for handicapped people only" stigma.

Well-meaning designers often create barrier-free oddities, visually segregating people with different abilities from the norm. Too many elderly people struggle up stairways rather than make a spectacle of themselves by using the open lift installed to meet their needs. Too many ramps have been attached as makeshift accommodations to meet code, destroying the appearance of a building while attracting unwanted attention to the user. Too many cumbersome aids have become institutional clichés, and too many people have been isolated by their use.

In an effort to meet differences in user needs, complicated modifications are often made to existing products. In many cases these modifications only serve to make the products more difficult to use. Rather than empowering the user by saving time and energy, these "technological dreams" become maintenance nightmares, consuming time that could be spent in more creative pursuits. The "user-unfriendly" contraptions intimidate rather than support, reinforcing a feeling of inadequacy. In the process, they become visual advertisements of disability or emblems of age.

Manufacturers seldom label their products as barrier-free or accessible, fearing that this would embarrass users or reduce sales to the general public. As a result, many helpful products are virtually unknown to the growing market of people with different abilities who could be well served by them. Many of these products are both functional and beautiful. In fact, the strict parameters of a barrier-free design may actually inspire purity of form, encouraging a designer to take a minimalist approach, which focuses attention on the user rather than on the equipment. "Beautiful" and "barrier-free" are not necessarily mutually exclusive terms.

The purpose of this book is to attract attention to the many design options that can be used in creative ways to meet the needs of all people. These design solutions transcend ability with innovation. The technology is in place, there is an enormous need, and with a little imagination designers and architects can literally free us from our handicaps, providing a world without barriers.

TARGETING THE LARGEST MARKET: PEOPLE WITH ARTHRITIS

One out of every five Americans needs help seeing, hearing, speaking, walking, using stairs, lifting, carrying objects, getting around, or simply getting out of bed. According to the Census Bureau, 37.4 million people need some type of assistance, and at least 31 million have arthritis.[2]

Most people with arthritis are not in wheelchairs. Instead, they have differences in mobility, including a slower walking speed, a forward center of gravity, a stooped posture, and reduced stamina. This population benefits from products that are ergonomically designed—for instance, bathtubs that are easy to get in and out of, chairs that allow the user to lean forward and push off, and textured floor surfaces that reduce slipping and provide greater traction. Buildings routes should be planned so that occupants are not required to walk long distances. Corridors and doorways should provide adequate space for mobility aids. Stairs should have appropriately designed handrails, treads, and risers.

People with arthritis often experience reduced strength, reach, and coordination. Joints may be more rigid, arm extension may be reduced, and muscle strength may be diminished. To prevent these differences from becoming handicaps, building designers must make modifications that address these physical limitations. Cabinets and other storage space, for example, should be located within easy reach. Controls should be able to be operated with a closed fist; levers should replace knobs, and push buttons should be used instead of dials. If furnishings, accessories, or appliances must be moved, lightweight models should be specified.

People with differences in strength, reach, and coordination need products that can prevent accidents and increase reaction time to emergencies. Grab bars and handrails should be placed strategically in rooms, and tables and other items should have rounded corners. To reduce accidental burns, appliances should be properly placed and fire-retardant materials should be used. Building systems should be planned to increase reaction time and to control fire, security breaches, and other emergency situations. Examples include smoke alarms, motion detectors that trigger exterior lighting, and call systems that can send help at the push of a button.

BUILDINGS THAT ENHANCE HEARING

An estimated 21 million people in the United States have hearing impairments.[3] Many have difficulty with high-frequency sounds and problems separating voices from background noise. Through appropriate building design, ambient and transmitted background noise can be reduced and static, which interferes with hearing aids, can be controlled.

Increased lighting and supportive furniture arrangements can facilitate lip reading and improve the ability to distinguish sign language. Redundant cuing (e.g., signals with lights and vibration as well as auditory cues) can improve communication for people who have differences in hearing.

DESIGNING FOR DIFFERENCES IN VISION

The 16 million Americans with differences in vision also profit from redundant cuing.[4] For example, raised numerals on office doors encourage tactile use, and chimes in elevators provide auditory cues to supplement vision. Vision differences become handicaps when insufficient contrast or illegible detail is specified. Many people with vision differences benefit from larger lettering on signs and controls, contrasting molding around doorways, and lighting systems with the flexibility to increase lighting quantity as needed. In providing for people with vision differences, designers and architects should allow for an increased number of defused lighting sources to reduce glare. Defusing finishes should be specified on floor, wall, ceiling, and furniture surfaces. Lighting transitions should be planned between light and dark areas to prevent the "dazzle" experienced when walking outdoors from a dark interior. Elevated protruding objects like spiral staircases should also be eliminated or modified. People who use canes cannot detect obstructions over 2 ft 3 in high and can easily walk into the sharp corner of a protruding stair.[5]

ENVIRONMENTS FOR MENTAL HEALTH

Little design research has been conducted in the field of mental health. It is known, though, that many people with mental differences have a diminished ability to process information and difficulty in relating to unfamiliar environments. In addition, they experience increased stress due to diminished function. Yet, like all of us, they have a strong desire for independence and security, as well as a strong need for social interaction. Environmental planning can increase stress management capabilities by offering a sense of control, access to social support, and positive distractions in the physical surroundings. Access to nature is an example of a positive distraction. In laboratory tests, visual exposure to nature produced significant recovery from stress within five minutes.[6]

Designers and architects can meet some mental health needs by controlling the amount of information and stimuli in the environment. Confusing signage, a noisy environment, and lack of planning for wayfinding and orientation all contribute to stress. Stress management and independence can be enhanced through design for efficacy, or the ability to control. Providing separate thermostats in patients' rooms, laundry room and kitchen access in hospitals, and choice of background music and artwork are examples of patient-centered design that return control to the individual.

Many people with mental differences take medications that may reduce strength, coordination, mobility, and stamina. For people on high doses of tranquilizers, for instance, each motion may seem as difficult as moving through a vat of molasses. Products should be specified that are inviting to use, require little physical energy, and are easy to maintain. A spa, for example, may be more inviting and easier to use than a bathtub or shower.

People with Alzheimer's disease and related dementias experience declining intellectual function, cognitive impairment, and loss of clear consciousness. Building designers can support both caregivers and patients by providing reference points to the past and present, a homelike environment with safe and secure exterior and interior spaces, and a consistent and relatively uncomplicated space that is easy to negotiate. All of these design criteria will offer patients a more independent lifestyle and more success in task accomplishment leading to an enhanced self-image.

WHEELCHAIR ACCESS

Much has been written about accessible design for the 2 million Americans in wheelchairs, but surprisingly little has been done, and even less has been done well.[7] Stairs abound and slopes on ramps exceed the minimum requirements of code. Maneuvering spaces are inadequate, and narrow doorways prevent access. Elaborate accessibility plans are substituted for good design; wheelchair users are forced into freight elevators where the garbage is frequently stored. They are assigned remote locations for entrance and exit, making an emergency escape next to impossible. Much of the storage in most buildings is out of reach, and those items that can be accessed may be difficult to use because of the angle of reach required from the wheelchair. Clear standards for design have been available for over 30 years and there are many examples of the freedom provided by accessible design, yet much remains to be done.

This is not another book on space planning for people in wheelchairs. The available design standards are excellent, but even when these standards are followed, it is often necessary for designers to exceed code to meet the requirements of their clients. Many people in wheelchairs, for instance, require a 5- by 5-ft turnaround space in public bathroom stalls, even though that space is not always specified in code. Others need the assistance of a spouse or aide, yet unisex bathrooms are seldom offered because they are not mandated. Door openings are often based on clearance of the wheelchair, not clearance of the elbows of the user.

DESIGN CONFLICTS

There are often conflicting design needs for different clients. For example, stronger people in wheelchairs can benefit from an automatic door closer. But the mechanism may prevent a weaker person from opening the door. Blind people who use canes may not detect an open upper cabinet door, but those who can use only one arm cannot access storage if the upper cabinet door has an automatic closer. People in wheelchairs must have curb cuts, but those cuts may make it difficult for blind people who use canes to determine if they are about to walk into traffic.

To add to the confusion, many clients have multiple disabilities. In addition to those mentioned above, clients may have problems with incontinence, sensation loss, or respiration difficulties, or may be in constant pain. Environments can be designed to provide support for such clients. For people with incontinence, for example, a bidet can be selected for use after a bowel and bladder program. For people with sensation loss, water temperature controls and hot water surge protectors can be used. For people with respiration difficulties, specialized controls for irritants, humidity, airflow, and temperature can be installed. For people in pain, easily adjustable beds and angled tabletops may provide comfortable support.

Although many products meet more than one need and are somewhat universal in application, it is important to study specific needs when targeting the barrier-free design market. This book can be used by designers and architects to present specific choices to clients, allowing end users to make the final decision whenever possible. Postoccupancy evaluation should also be pursued on barrier-free design projects with users evaluating the finished installation.

AGING IN PLACE

With the many reductions in federal participation in housing and an expanding elderly population, today's barrier-free designs may well become the housing option of the future, permitting aging in place. Sixty percent of all disabilities occur after age 60.[8] Eighty percent of elderly people suffer from chronic limitation of mobility.[9] Forty-eight percent have arthritis, 29 percent have hearing difficulties, 17 percent have orthopedic impairments, and 14 percent have vision problems.[10] With medical science extending the life span, it is estimated that there will be over 65 million people over the age of 65 by the year 2030.[11] The fastest-growing demand for barrier-free design may well be found in the aging population. In 1988 alone, senior citizens were estimated to be an $800 billion market.[12]

In targeting this market, designers need to remember that seniors will resist products that make them feel different or isolated from the norm. They will value designs that enhance and simplify their lives, making activities easier and more enjoyable. Products that create activity may actually be preferred over products that save time.[13] Such confusing gadgets as answering machines, videocassette recorders, and automatic teller machines are examples of time-saving products that are often avoided by elderly people.

ECONOMIC REALITIES OF BARRIER-FREE DESIGN

For the purposes of the Internal Revenue Service, many barrier-free products and designs are legitimate medical expenses that can be deducted if they exceed 7$\frac{1}{2}$ percent of an individual's adjusted gross income.[14] Examples include grab bars, widened doorways, and ramps.

Businesses may deduct up to $15,000 of the cost of complying with the Americans with Disabilities Act. Small businesses may be eligible for tax credits on some of these costs. On the other hand, the cost of not complying with ADA may be a lawsuit. According to the Rand Corporation, the average cost of fighting this kind of suit is $250,000.[15]

Some barrier-free design expenses are reimbursable through public and private insurance programs. In addition, some states offer aid and low-interest loans through community development block grants and similar programs. The Paralyzed Veterans of America also offers grants to qualified applicants.

For some types of projects, accessibility may add as little as 1 percent to the total project cost of new construction.[16] These low costs are achieved in large-scale commercial facilities when accessibility is considered as an initial design objective. In a housing study by the National Association of Home Builders,[17] full compliance with the American National Standards Institute A117.1-1986 requires between 6 percent and 14.5 percent additional space in most units with corresponding cost increases; remodeling to comply with ANSI can be even more expensive. As an example of the costs of new construction, recently an accessible home in Louisville, Colorado, cost $182,000 for 1900 square feet, about $15,000 more than a nonaccessible model. Universal and adaptable housing will be significantly less expensive than full compliance with ANSI. With these homes, accessibility features are added as needed to keep initial costs to a minimum.

Although many of the products and design ideas selected for this book are well priced, they were chosen primarily for their innovative qualities, not for their low cost. Some are available in less expensive models, and others will be offered at reduced prices as demand increases. Affordability and accessibility need not be mutually exclusive.

A data base listing alternative products has been developed. A computer search can be conducted to locate replacements for products which do not meet budget requirements or which are no longer available. Details are provided adjacent to the reference list of manufacturers in the back of this book.

Acknowledgments

Beautiful Barrier-Free could not have been produced without the efforts of Susan Behar, ASID. The hundreds of interiors and products that are illustrated in this book were culled by Susan from thousands of examples. Her selection decisions were based on years of professional training, as well as on her personal experiences with her daughter, Jessie, who has inspired her many contributions to the field of barrier-free design. In a like manner, my brother, Eric Hildebrand, has inspired me with his brave and faithful battle with mental illness.

I would also like to acknowledge the work of Bettyann Boetticher Raschko. Her research has become the standard of our field, and without it this book would not have been possible.

Special thanks go to the many colleagues who volunteered their time to critique this book. Beulah Wayne offered the benefit of her experience in a wheelchair, reviewing the book from her perspective. John Salmen, AIA, a pioneer in barrier-free design, offered helpful criticism over the 10-year production period. His contributions in exterior planning, ramps, stairs, elevators, and electrical, mechanical, and accoustical equipment are gratefully acknowledged. Patricia Ray, IBD, a nationally recognized expert in the specification of carpeting and hard surface flooring, carefully reviewed the chapter on floor covering. William L. Wilkoff, FASID, IBD, provided thoughtful guidance and friendship throughout the production process. Kenneth W. Smith, CKD, CBD, a leader in the field of kitchen and bath design, evaluated the kitchen and bath chapters, and S. C. Reznikoff, CSI, reviewed portions of the book dealing with flammability. Jill Boice offered technical expertise on modifications to support hearing and speech. Vija Berzins is gratefully acknowledged for her contribution to the graphic design of the book.

Thank you to Jain Malkin for support of my work and for her referral to Van Nostrand Reinhold. VNR's entire staff has been a source of unending assistance, with special accolades going to Amanda Miller for her calm guidance through the publishing process. In addition to the editorial staff at VNR, I thank my husband for the hours of editing and rewriting that he contributed to this project.

I would like to acknowledge the support of my colleagues at Colorado State University. Through the dedication and leadership of Don Sherman, FIDEC, and through years of encouragement by Craig Birdsong, IDEC, this book has become a reality.

I am especially indebted to Wayne Ruga, AIA, ISID, for serving as my mentor and as an example of leadership in our field, and to the National Symposium on Healthcare Design for support of much of the research cited in this book.

Icon Guide

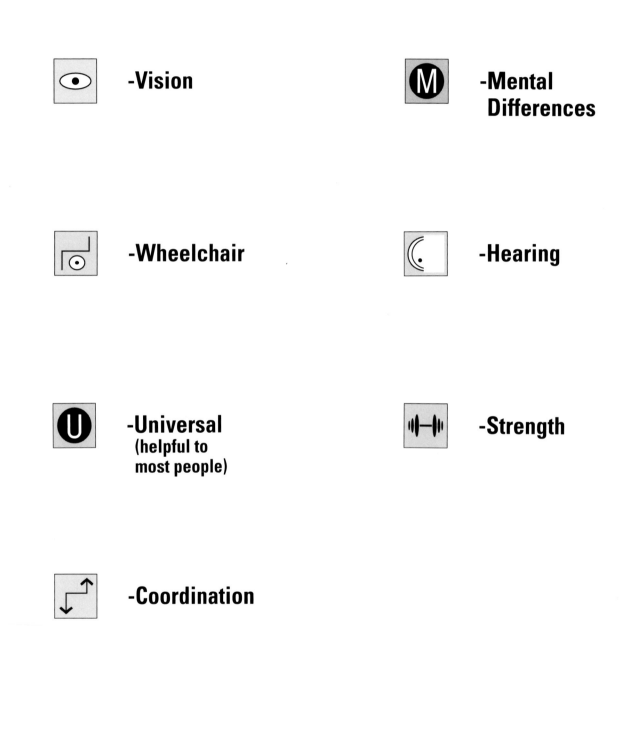

-Vision

-Mental
Differences

-Wheelchair

-Hearing

-Universal
(helpful to
most people)

-Strength

-Coordination

1. Exterior Planning, Ramps, Stairs, and Elevators

Ⓤ Accessibility should be the measure of good design rather than the exception to the norm. It should be expected that any well-designed building would provide the minimal amenities of an accessible approach, a supportive site, and landscaping that can be enjoyed by all people with differences in ability.

Ⓤ Emblems of age and disability are often specified by well-meaning designers attempting to make a building accessible. Temporary ramps, attached as an afterthought, advertise the differences of those who must use them and detract from the exterior appearance of the building. Open lifts segregate users from those who are able to negotiate the adjacent stairs. Often visitors choose to struggle with stairs rather than deal with the spectacle of a ride on the lift. Elevators close in the face of those who need a little more time. Steep ramps and inadequate handrails frighten people away.

EXTERIOR PLANNING

Ⓤ Building accessibility begins with a covered entry at each exterior doorway, which will be appreciated by anyone who is looking for keys or waiting for a ride. Outdoor seating in this area is also helpful. Plan the entry with a slip-resistant surface that drains away from the door. An exception to this rule is a ramp landing (which must be level). The entry should be protected from wind to allow the door to be easily opened. (Fig. 1-1) A drop-off area is preferable and should be visible from the front door. A minimum vertical clearance of 9 ft 6 in is needed by some vans.[1]

1-1

Plan a well-lighted access aisle in all parking areas or garages for transfer to a car or van. People who transfer to a car equipped with hand controls require a 5-ft clear space to completely open the car door. (Fig. 1-2). Those using a perpendicular side lift on a van will require a wide aisle (8 ft) adjacent to an 8-ft parking space.[2] The space should be level (not exceeding a slope of 1:50 in all directions).[3] An accessible route free of auto traffic and protected from adverse weather elements should be provided. (Fig. 1-3) It can be a minimum of 3 ft in width except at narrow turns. (Fig. 1-4).

Provide seating and resting places on longer routes. Street furniture and equipment should be recessed into alcoves. Water fountains, benches, waste receptacles, telephones, and other overhanging objects may be obstacles to people with differences in vision. Signs with raised letters or braille symbols are important, as are auditory cues. Maps of the parking area are helpful, especially to people with differences in hearing or speech who may be hesitant to ask for directions. (Fig. 1-5) Install adequate lighting for map use and crime prevention.

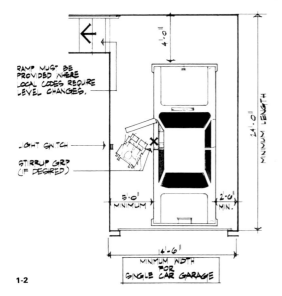

1-2

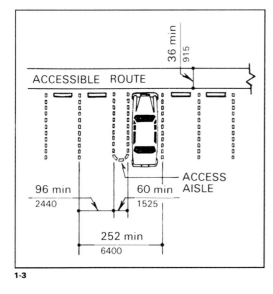

1-3

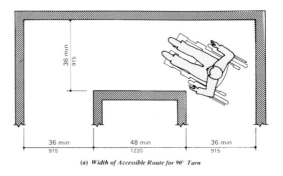

(a) Width of Accessible Route for 90° Turn

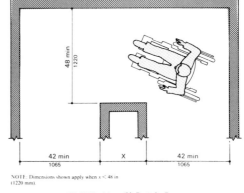

NOTE: Dimensions shown apply when x < 48 in (1220 mm).

(b) Width of Accessible Route for Turns around an Obstruction

1-4

1-5

1-6

1-7

U Parking spaces for people with different abilities should be located as close as possible to an accessible entrance. An accessible sign[4] should clearly designate parking. (Fig. 1-6)

U Attach the garage on the same level as the main building. When planning a residence for a person in a wheelchair, include a covered two-car garage to protect the client, as well as an attendant or guest. In commercial spaces, plan a covered connection between buildings. (Fig. 1-7)

U A quiet building site is necessary for people with differences in hearing, as well as for people who are differently sighted who rely more on their sense of hearing. People with speech differences also need quiet spaces in which they can be heard easily. Select a site away from major roads, airports, and railroads. Windows and doors should be oriented away from any sources of noise adjacent to the site. (Fig. 1-8) In existing construction, earth berms and exterior plants can be placed in front of windows and doors to buffer noise. An earth berm can also be used as a ramp.

1-8

1-9

1-10

U Elevated gardens are convenient for gardeners who get stiff while kneeling or for people in wheelchairs. (Fig. 1-9) Pots and planters should be at least 2 ft in height and should be accessible from both sides if they exceed a 2-ft depth. They can be mounted on stands, walls, or racks. (Fig. 1-10) Specify nontoxic plants to protect children, pets, and people with allergies.

U Flowerpots and baskets can be suspended by a pulley system that allows them to be lowered for watering and pruning. An alternative method for watering is a drip irrigation system. In addition, carts and watering wands can be used with gardening activities. A vertical garden offers easy access to plants. One version, featured by the Chicago Botanical Gardens, consists of a coarse screen mounted loosely to a wall. The screen is lined with sphagnum, filled with potting soil, and planted through holes cut in the screen.

U Patios offer sheltered gardening. They also provide an area in which to move the bed outdoors. This is very important to people who spend their time in bed. Patios should be covered and extend into an accessible escape route. (Fig. 1-11)

1-11

U Plan a covered exterior route for emergency escapes. Such a route usually consists of a covered sidewalk around the perimeter of the building. For security and safety, the sidewalk should be well lighted. It should be adequately drained yet free of gratings, which could catch on wheels and crutches. Gratings used in other areas should have spaces no greater than $1/2$ in wide. (Fig. 1-12)

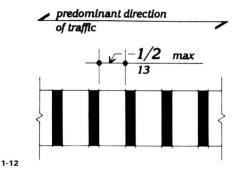

1-12

U Brick, sand, and cobblestoned surfaces are examples of textures that are difficult for many people. Abrupt edges and drops in the sidewalk pose a tripping hazard and a barrier for people in wheelchairs. Specify adequate drainage and sidewalk subbase construction to prevent settling and the resulting changes in level. Ramp existing changes of level exceeding $1/2$ in. Bevel changes of level between $1/4$ in and $1/2$ in.[5]

U Where an accessible route crosses a curb, provide a curb ramp built to the Americans with Disabilities Act Accessibility Guidelines (ADAAG) in slope, location, width, and surface.[6] Curb ramps should not extend into the accessible route. When a curb ramp is cut into the level accessible route, the resulting slope can pull people in wheelchairs out into the street. (Fig. 1-13)

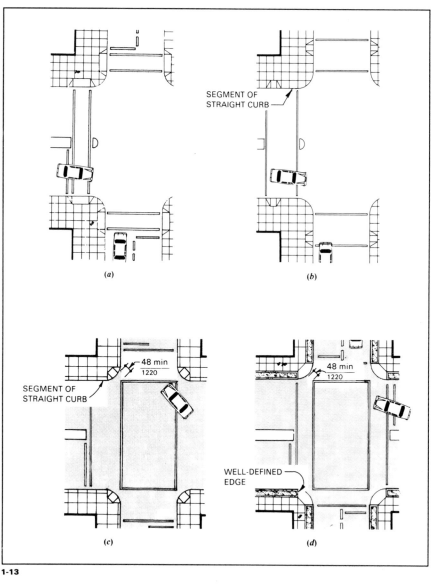

1-13

U Specify flared sides on curb ramps since steep sides can pose a tripping hazard to pedestrians. (Fig. 1-14). Curb ramps can also be a hazard to people with differences in vision who use curb edges to signal the beginning of the street. Use a uniform textural cue to prevent this problem. (Fig. 1-15). Also use texture on sidewalk intersections that lead directly into the street or parking lot.

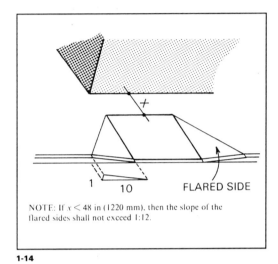

NOTE: If $x < 48$ in (1220 mm), then the slope of the flared sides shall not exceed 1:12.

1-14

DETECTABLE WARNING

DETECTABLE WARNING

1-15

RAMPS

Unless the design appears to be an integral part of the architecture, permanent ramps attached to a home may reduce the resale value and limit prospective buyers. Wood or metal ramps are easy to dismantle. Wood ramps are also easier to build and can be modified if mistakes are made in construction. Use fire-retardant wood that has been pressure treated (or is decay-resistant, like redwood). Hot dip galvanized bolts and screws (with washers) should be used to resist corrosion. (Fig. 1-16)

If properly installed, pebble-grained roll roofing makes a good nonskid surface for fire-retardant wood ramps. Commercial nonskid floor coverings are also appropriate. Do not specify carpet for ramps, especially indoor/outdoor carpeting which may become slippery when wet. Sheet vinyl and painted surfaces are also slippery when wet or dusty, but ribbed rubber matting works well. Install the ribs to run across the width of the ramp.

1-16

Permanent concrete ramps are usually more expensive than wood, but concrete ramps are easier to maintain and last longer. Specify a sand-float or broom finish brushed across the slope, not with it, to prevent slipping. A broom finish is also easier for blind people who use a cane. Avoid exterior ramps in climates with ice and snow, or cover them with a canopy. Built-in electric heating coils can also be considered.

Portable ramps are the least expensive method, but they can be too steep for many people to use. If the ramp is 3 ft in length and used on a 6-in step, the client must negotiate a 1:6 slope. Be aware that this is twice as steep as ramps built to ADAAG standards.

If the ramp will be dedicated to wheelchair use, base the slope of the ramp on the ability of the client to negotiate it. To meet minimum standards, the slope of an interior or exterior ramp should not exceed 1 in of rise for every 1 ft of length and the cross slope should be less than 1 in for every 4 ft 2 in of width. The ramp should not exceed 30 ft in length without a landing. If possible, use a shorter ramp with a more gradual slope. (Fig. 1-17)

Curbs 2 in high should be considered on both sides of the ramp to serve as guardrails for wheels. Use low curbs instead of sidewalls to prevent scrapes and bumps. Handrails can be used by both pedestrians and people in wheelchairs who pull themselves up the ramp. Ramp handrails should meet ADAAG requirements. Handrails should always be installed on both sides of a ramp if the ramp has a rise greater than 6 in (and a length greater than 6 ft). (Fig. 1-18) Shorter ramps without handrails should have flared sides to prevent tripping accidents.

The flat landings at the beginning and end of the ramp and at any turnaround point should be 5 ft in length.

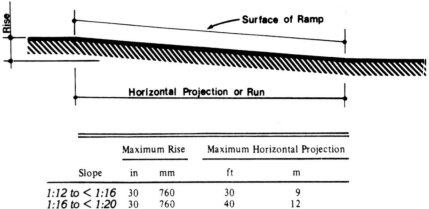

1-17

| | Maximum Rise | | Maximum Horizontal Projection | |
Slope	in	mm	ft	m
1:12 to < 1:16	30	760	30	9
1:16 to < 1:20	30	760	40	12

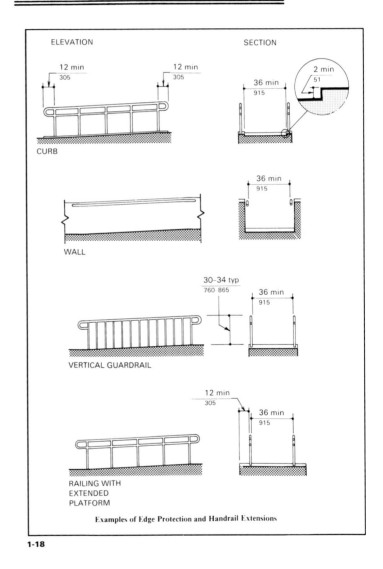

Examples of Edge Protection and Handrail Extensions

1-18

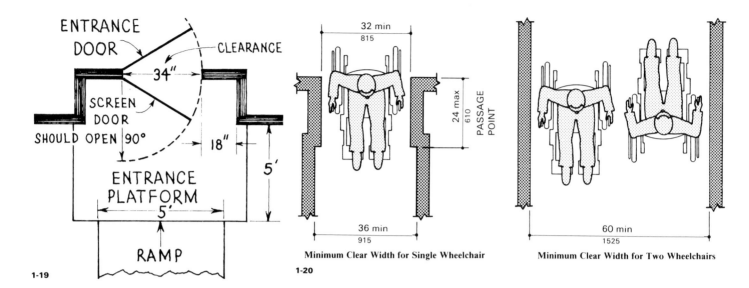

1-19

Minimum Clear Width for Single Wheelchair

1-20

Minimum Clear Width for Two Wheelchairs

When the door opens onto the ramp, the entrance platform should extend 18 in on the side next to the door handle so that the door can be opened without backing up a wheelchair. The ramp should be directed toward the handle side of the door if the door opens onto the ramp. If the door opens into the house, orient the ramp to the hinge side of the door. (Fig. 1-19)

The width should be a minimum of 3 ft for one-way traffic including wheelchairs, 4 ft for two-way ambulatory traffic, and 5 ft for two wheelchairs to pass. (Fig. 1-20)

A ramp into a swimming pool should not exceed a slope of 1 ft of rise per 10 ft of length.[7] It should be 3 ft wide with railings on each side, which can be used to guide a shower chair upon entering and exiting. A portable lifting device can be used in place of a ramp. (Fig. 1-21)

1-21

1-22

U A series of steps can also be used to access a pool, with the highest step planned at wheelchair seat height (usually 19 in).[8] [In one creative installation, steps were replaced with a series of smooth rocks that is incorporated into the design.] (Fig. 1-22)

U An accessible 4-ft route should be planned around the pool. Both the ramp and the route should have a nonslip surface. (Fig. 1-23)

1-23

LIFTS, ELEVATORS, AND STAIRS

Lifts and Elevators

 A wheelchair lift or inclined elevator can be adapted to existing stairs. (Fig. 1-24) Some lifts are designed to hold a wheelchair and do not require a transfer. On a lift with a door, specify a locking device that prevents the lift from moving unless the door is locked. The lift should be designed to protect against entrapment under the platform and any failure that could cause the platform to drop. A slippery or jolting platform may cause the user to lose his or her balance. A closed installation is required for any application exceeding two stories.

 If the lift requires a transfer into a seat, a second wheelchair must be in place at the other end. Wheelchair lift seats store at the bottom of the stairs to permit unobstructed use of the stairway. Folding seats are also available. If a lift requires a separate power unit, be sure it does not block the accessible route. (Fig. 1-25)

U Freight elevators are not reasonable accommodations for people in wheelchairs, and both ADAAG and the Uniform Federal Accessibility Standards (UFAS) prohibit their use to meet accessibility requirements. On an accessible elevator, a minimum interior size of 4 ft 6 in by 5 ft 8 in should be maintained, but a 4 ft by 4 ft interior meets code in some situations. (Fig. 1-26)

1-25

1-24

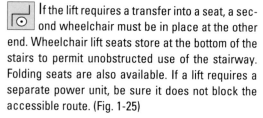

NOTE: Elevator cars with a minimum width less than that shown above, but no less than 54 in (1370 mm), are allowed for elevators with capacities of less than 2000 lb. A center opening door application necessitates increasing the 68-in (1730-mm) dimension to 80 in (2030 mm).

Minimum Dimensions of Elevator Cars

1-26

The elevator should be automatic and self-leveling (within a tolerance of $1/2$ in). Leveling should be tested with a full load as well as without a load.[9] The elevator should start and stop smoothly, and a fold-down seat and stationary handrail should be provided for use by people with differences in balance and strength.

A visual indicator on each elevator control button should light when touched and extinguish when the command is completed. All car controls, as well as the car platform, landing sill, and car threshold, should be illuminated to at least five foot-candles.[10] Position indicators should incorporate redundant cuing, offering both visual and audible cues. In the hall, an audible signal should sound once for the up direction and twice for the down (or use a verbal announcement of up or down).

Call buttons should be installed at a maximum height of 3 ft 6 in, with the up button on top. Consider a second call button for short people or children installed at a height between 2 ft 10 in and 3 ft.[11] Any object placed or installed beneath the call buttons should not project into the space more than 4 in.[12] A call button should be a minimum of $3/4$ in in diameter. Hall lanterns, indicating which car is answering the call, should be a minimum of $2^1/2$ in in diameter. In addition, a 2-in-high raised floor designation should be mounted to the hoistway entrance. It should be installed at a height of 5 ft, and a second designation should be installed at 3 ft 4 in for children.[13] (Fig. 1-27)

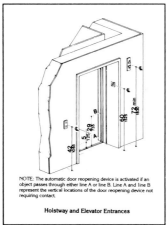

NOTE: The automatic door reopening device is activated if an object passes through either line A or line B. Line A and line B represent the vertical locations of the door reopening device not requiring contact.

Hoistway and Elevator Entrances

1-27

Interior control panels should be installed within reach from a wheelchair. (Fig. 1-28) Controls for children should be installed at a height of 3 ft.[14] Some panels are designed to be mounted horizontally to improve reach. Arrange the numbers in ascending order, reading from left to right. A floor number or other raised designation should be installed to the left of the button and should contrast with the background. (Fig. 1-29) Numerals above the door should illuminate, and a signal should sound as the car passes or stops at a floor. A verbal announcement may be substituted for the signal. Specify a signal of no less than 20 dB, with a frequency no higher than 1500 Hz.[15]

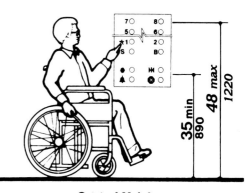

1-28   **Control Height**

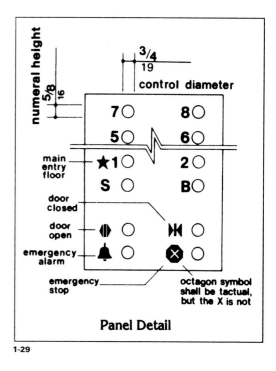

Panel Detail

1-29

Ⓤ The elevator should have a sound signal to indicate that it is safe to enter or exit. If the door becomes obstructed, it should reopen without requiring contact and remain open for at least 20 seconds.[16] ADAAG and UFAS require only that a door remain open for as little as 5 seconds in response to a call. This is insufficient time for many people to respond, even if forewarned of arrival by redundant cuing.

Ⓤ In addition, there should be an emergency communication system inside the car complying with ADAAG in height, hardware, and length of cord, if any. A verbal system (like an intercom) should be incorporated in addition to an alarm system. Intercoms are easier to use and tougher to vandalize than systems requiring the use of a handset. Only the nonverbal alarm system is required, however. Instructions for use should be both tactile and visual.

Stairs

People with mobility differences have difficulty negotiating spiral or curved staircases, which require balance and dependence on the handrails. Straight staircases must provide a safe stopping place midway between floor levels to help those who are prone to dizziness or those who need to conserve energy. A seat on the landing is helpful to many. (Fig. 1-30)

1-30

1-31

U A handrail of 1½-in diameter allows the strongest and most comfortable grip. It should have rounded ends or return to the wall or floor, and should not extend into the pedestrian pathway by more than 4 in.[17] A handrail should also clear the adjacent wall by 1½ in. Many people place their entire lower arm on the handrail to push up; the arm can become wedged between the wall and the rail if a larger clearance is allowed. To prevent scraped knuckles, the wall surface behind the handrail should not be textured. Texture can be used on the handrail itself for improved grip and orientation. Notches or grooves can be cut in the rail to identify location. Handrails should not rotate within their fittings. They should be installed on both sides and should not end in the corners. They should be continuous on the inner rail at switchbacks and doglegs. Mount handrails for accessible ramps and stairs at a height of 2 ft 10 in to 3 ft 2 in above the stair nosing or ramp surface.[18] A lower handrail can be installed at a height of 26 in for use by children. It should have a diameter of 1¼ in.[19] (Fig. 1-31)

U A handrail can be recessed to a maximum of 3 in if the recess extends at least 18 in above the top of the rail.[20] It should extend 12 in beyond the top and 12 in plus the width of one riser beyond the bottom of stairs and ramps. At the bottom, the handrail should continue to slope for a distance of the width of one tread. The remaining 12 in should be horizontal. (Fig. 1-32)

People with balance problems may be able to manage steps more easily than ramps. Do not design steps with abrupt or square nosings or open risers; open risers are nearly impossible for people with canes or other mobility aids to use. Use wedge-shaped fillers on existing square nosings.

For people with differences in motion, keep every riser at the same height and every tread at 11 in deep in any flight of stairs.[21] Tread width should also be consistent within each flight. (Fig. 1-33)

To prevent people from walking into a hanging stairway or other elevated protruding object, install wing walls in front of it. Guardrails or planters could also be used to block the side of the hanging stairway. (Fig. 1-34)

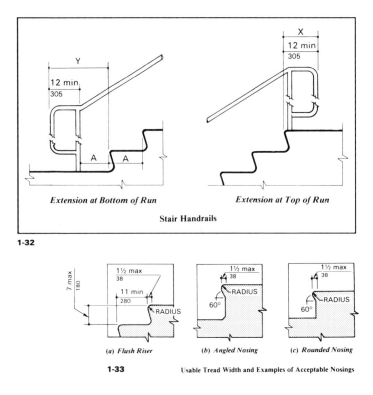

Extension at Bottom of Run   *Extension at Top of Run*

Stair Handrails

1-32

(a) *Flush Riser*   (b) *Angled Nosing*   (c) *Rounded Nosing*

1-33   Usable Tread Width and Examples of Acceptable Nosings

1-34

On stairs, color contrast treads and risers so that the edges can be spotted more easily. Also contrast the handrails from the wall so that they can be seen more quickly in an emergency. (Fig. 1-35)

Single stairs can be difficult to see and are dangerous when they are not expected or lighted properly. A change in texture or color on a single stair will help. Texture should also be used to mark stairway entrances and other areas that are hazardous to people with differences in vision.

Braces and other mobility aids can abrade the edges of carpeted stairs. On a straight staircase, cut the carpet long enough to allow an extra riser of carpet to be tucked under at the bottom of the carpet runner. When the edges show wear, the entire piece can be rotated so that the worn edge can be hidden in the intersection between each tread and riser. When using hard-surface flooring on stairs, specify edge guards.

1-35

2. Electrical, Mechanical, and Acoustical Equipment

From door levers that double as night-lights to sophisticated "smart house" systems, technology can enable seniors to live independently. Low-voltage lighting, for example, can serve as a guide through confusing spaces. HVAC systems can customize the environment and come complete with redundantly cued thermostats that almost anyone can use. Why aren't more people making use of the modern technology? Are there too many choices? Are the changes happening too fast? Are people afraid that they can't handle the technology?

Maybe it's just that many devices call attention to the fact that the user needs special help. The challenge of the designer is to apply sophisticated technology to solve problems without drawing attention to individual differences. Discriminating architecture does not discriminate.

SWITCHES

The lower location of electrical switches is a top priority in planning for wheelchair access, but lower switches are also helpful for children and for elderly people who lean forward and naturally gaze downward. Locate light switches at the height of the door lever (2 ft 6 in for use by people in wheelchairs and by small children).[1] If small children are present, the thermostat must be placed higher up (4 ft 6 in), even though the control may be hard to reach from a wheelchair. To approach a switch from a wheelchair, provide an open floor space (2 ft 6 in by 4 ft) in front of each switch, and plan an accessible route.

2-1

2-2

Switches must be placed for convenience as well as for ease of access. In rooms longer than 15 ft, plan switches in more than one location. In lecture halls, plan light switches that can be controlled by the lecturer from the front of the room. To save unnecessary trips, plan a master switch at both the back door and at bedside to control all lights in a residence. Sound-activated switches can be helpful to control fixtures that are out of reach. These switches come on with a clap of the hands and can be a great help for people with differences in vision or those who just want to save steps. Timer switches are also convenient and are especially good choices for outside lighting.

In bedrooms, consider a lighted switch that can act as a beacon in the dark. People with differences in sight appreciate rheostats on each switch to control the quantity of light in the room. A rheostat is also helpful for task lighting. (Fig. 2-1) For example, it may be necessary to increase lighting over the kitchen sink or in other areas where detailed work takes place.

Thermostats with braille and high-contrast numbers are helpful for people with vision differences. A control that features an audible click between settings can be helpful. (Fig. 2-2). In the bedroom, heating, cooling, ventilation, and remote controls should be placed conveniently near the bed but should not be near a heat register, which could affect the temperature reading. Keep all controls at a uniform level except those that could be hazardous to young children; place the latter at a height of 4 ft 6 in.

Ⓤ Make sure the main switch box is installed in an accessible area. If the switch box location is not well lighted, add a magnetic flashlight on the box. Use circuit breakers rather than fuses, which may be more difficult for people with arthritis to handle. Label all circuits, and keep the top of the box at a reachable height (4 ft 6 in) for a side approach in a wheelchair.

Ⓤ Wall-mount kitchen fan controls or use a fan mounted on the counter with controls within reach. (Fig. 2-3). Wall-mount the switch for the bathroom light outside the bathroom. It is always helpful to have lighting before negotiating a confined space.

Wall guards may be necessary around some switches where dirt and stains are a problem. Specify palm toggle switches, which can be operated with the elbow or a closed fist. (Fig. 2-4). Pressure or rocker-type switches are easier to operate than conventional toggle switches. Pull chains are easy to handle if a loop is attached to the end of the chain so that grasping is not necessary.

Ⓤ Projecting switch plates are easier to locate in areas with reduced lighting. Self-illuminated trim for switches and levers are also helpful and should be installed at bedroom, bathroom, and entry doors. (Fig. 2-5) It may be necessary to add nightlights as well. Low-voltage lighting on the floor surface can aid in wayfinding. (Fig. 2-6)

2-3

2-5

2-4

2-6

2-7

2-8

Ⓤ Color contrast between the plate and the wall makes the switch easier to see. (Fig. 2-7). Contrast between the switch and the plate is also helpful.

OUTLETS

Ⓤ For small appliances, install an outlet just above the surface of a countertop or table. For the hair dryer or shaver, add an electrical outlet on the side wall of the bathroom, with a ground fault circuit interrupter to protect against shock. (Fig. 2-8) People in wheelchairs and others with mobility problems may have difficulty bending; electric cords on the floor, then, cannot be retrieved easily. Cup hooks next to an outlet can be a temporary solution to the problem, but a face plate that holds an unplugged cord would be better. (Fig. 2-9)

2-9

Ⓤ Extension cords can pose a tripping hazard and can become entangled in wheelchairs. To eliminate cords, add receptacle outlets to the floor plan after considering furniture, appliance, and lamp placement. Determine if additional outlets will be needed in the bedroom for such things as medical appliances, communication systems, and alarms. A special outlet, for example, may be necessary for recharging an electric wheelchair. Locate such an outlet in a well-ventilated area where noxious gases from charging will not build up. An outlet above an exterior door allows a call light or alarm to be added at a later date. In addition to the primary power source, a crucial call system should have a backup battery source.

U Electrical outlets must be accessible; a height of 15 in is preferable.[2] (Fig. 2-10) Make sure there is a receptacle outlet on the landing of all stairways for vacuuming. In rooms, outlets should be spaced within reach of most cords (no farther than 8 ft apart).

U Flexibility is the key to design for a variety of different abilities. Plan additional phone jacks, raceway outlets, (Fig. 2-11) and antenna hookups. In the kitchen, locate multiple outlets on the front of the counter for easier reach. Some appliances may even need an outlet under the counter. For example, a mixer could be stored under the counter on a pop-up shelf.

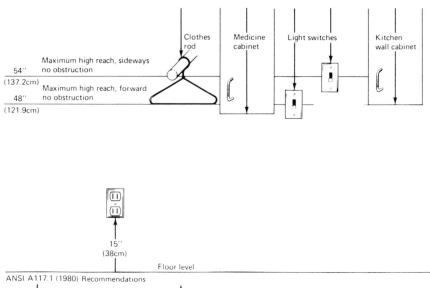

54″ (137.2cm) Maximum high reach, sideways no obstruction

48″ (121.9cm) Maximum high reach, forward no obstruction

Clothes rod   Medicine cabinet   Light switches   Kitchen wall cabinet

15″ (38cm)

Floor level

ANSI A117.1 (1980) Recommendations

Note: ↓ Denotes maximum height permitted, ↑ denotes minimum height permitted

2-10   ANSI A117.1 (1980) recommendations denoting minimum and maximum height of various components. (ANSI A117.1-1980)

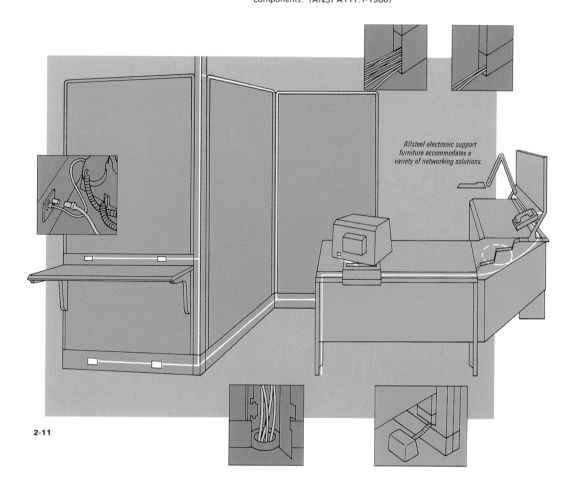

Allsteel electronic support furniture accommodates a variety of networking solutions.

2-11

2-12

2-13

LIGHTING

U Keep wall fixtures within reach and choose ceiling fixtures that pull down for bulb replacement. (Fig. 2-12) Those that cannot be lowered should be installed with long-life bulbs.

U Extra lighting is helpful when taking a shower from a shower chair or seat. Recess a vapor-proof light fixture in the ceiling of any shower stall. The light can be combined with an exhaust fan. (Fig. 2-13)

U Keep lighting consistent from room to room. Keep corridor lighting levels low at night.[3] Many people have trouble adjusting to sudden changes from light to dark areas. Create a transition zone, such as a well-lighted entryway or porch between the outdoors and the interior. Put side lights at the entrance to a bright room. Side lights and other accent lighting (instead of flat fluorescent light) can help people to maintain orientation within the room. Use shades or diffusers on all sources to prevent glare. Glare increases the deterioration rate of the retina,[4] and unprotected bulbs have high temperature surfaces capable of carbonizing dust, a source of irritation to many people with allergies.[5]

U Place lighting (and windows) to throw light toward, not down, staircases. (Fig. 2-14). Use a diffused source to prevent glare, not a directed source (e.g., a spotlight). Stairways and landings, especially the head and foot of the stairs, are potentially dangerous areas. If these spaces are dark, the pupils will dilate and it will be more difficult to focus. Keep the quantity of light adjustable throughout the entire space. Many elderly people require 4 to $5\frac{1}{2}$ times more light to distinguish a figure from the background (at least 100 fc for close work).[6] If lighting quantity increases, be careful to avoid excessive heat by using low-heat output luminaires.

2-14

Additional lighting is also important in areas where concentration is required, decisions are made, or danger is present. Decision areas, like a reception room and entryway, may require increased lighting. (Fig. 2-15) Many accidents occur in the kitchen and bathroom, so extra lighting becomes critical to accident prevention.

Glare is a problem for many people, including the elderly and people with vision problems. Use diffusers on light fixtures, and provide several low-intensity light sources rather than one bright source. Keep lights high and well diffused over the task area. Use low-glare surfaces on counters, floors, furnishings, and walls. Control window glare with draperies.

For people with hearing differences, plan adequate lighting to allow facial expressions, body movements, and gestures to be distinguished. Avoid backlighting and shadows on speakers and interpreters. Since flashing lights may be part of a warning system for hearing-impaired people, install light switches both inside and outside rooms requiring privacy, such as a bathroom.

Several factors must be considered when using fluorescent lighting. First, flickering fluorescent lights have been linked to triggering epileptic episodes. Second, hyperactive children and some people with concentration differences may experience a shortened attention span and nutritional problems triggered by fluorescent lighting.[7] Third, studies have shown that Alzheimer's patients and emotionally disturbed adolescents become more agitated under fluorescent lighting.[8] Fourth, flickering fluorescent lighting may interfere with hearing aids. Finally, cool fluorescent light emphasizes the blue-green tones that are most difficult to perceive for people with cataracts.[9] When planning fluorescent lighting, keep in mind that a lighting spectrum as close as possible to daylight may reduce depression, fatigue, hyperactivity, and some incidences of disease. The daylight spectrum also may increase calcium absorption and reaction time to light and sound.[10] This, in turn, may increase productivity. When using fluorescent tubes, specify a color spectrum similar to daylight. The ultraviolet light in the spectrum is also helpful in sanitizing the space for people with allergies.[11] (Fig. 2-16)

2-15

2-16

U Lighting design can help establish a feeling of intimacy and control. Efficacy is especially important to people with a variety of different abilities. Intimacy is created by lighting the perimeter walls of a room and keeping the center darker. People will feel more comfortable and will sit closer together without feeling as if they are "invading" each other's territory. (Fig. 2-17)

U Track lighting allows the quality and quantity of light to be altered as the client's needs change. With track lighting, the angle of the beam, the light color, and the light fixture can all be easily adjusted. For a change, light can be directed away from the ceiling of the room, creating a more personal feeling in the space. (Fig. 2-18). For example, kitchen fixtures can be directed at hanging cabinets to keep the light level below ceiling height without creating glare. Track lighting can be used to graze light over rough surfaces, to frame a painting in light (using a projector), or to change the location of a chandelier.

Mood	Lighting
Gaiety	Higher levels of illumination with color and movement. Changing effects of color and changes in illumination should not be sudden, but should be smooth and stimulating.
Solemnity	Subdued patterns of light with emphasis at dramatic points. Color should be used sparingly and with atmospheric effect. Changes of illumination should be imperceptible.
Restfulness	Low brightness patterns, no visible light sources, subdued color, dark upper ceiling, and a low wall brightness, decreasing upward to the ceiling.
Activity	Higher levels of illumination, with proper local lighting for the more difficult visual tasks.
Warmth	Colors at the red end of spectrum: red, red-orange, orange, yellow, amber, gold, and pink.
Coolness	Colors at cool end of spectrum, such as blue, blue-green, green, magenta, and violet. These colors mixed with white produces various cool tints.
Human Complexion	Light tints of red, such as pink and rose, improve human complexion and produce pleasant effects. Blue, blue-green, purple, and green detract from the human complexion, and produce ghastly effects.
Dramatize Color of Object	Spotlight by a beam of light of same color.
Prevent Fatigue	Avoid use of intense red, blue, or purple light.

NASA. *Habitability Data Handbook.* MSC-03909. p. 3-18.

2-17

2-18

U A less institutional appearance is achieved when only the light is seen, not the source of the light. Exposed lighting systems are often harsh and glaring and can visually take over a space. With concealed lighting systems, the emphasis is placed on the beauty of the room and its occupants, rather than on the light fixtures. Concealed fixtures are often less expensive than decorative fixtures. Concealed systems can be used to backlight wall accessories, to diffuse light on draperies, or to light the ceiling. (Fig. 2-19) Under-cabinet lighting can illuminate matte finish counters without glare.

U Recessed lighting under stairs prevents accidents without creating glare. Low-voltage lighting strips can be added to stairway floor coverings as an alternative treatment, but ensure that they are not visually confusing. (Fig. 2-20)

HEATING

U The type of heating system specified is important in meeting the needs of people with various differences and sensitivities. Electric baseboard heaters and hot water radiators offer even heating without drafts. Fluid-filled electric radiant heating is often advantageous for people with allergies, since the relatively low surface temperatures of these systems do not carbonize dust.[12] For people who cannot easily sense heat, warm radiators must be covered to prevent burns. This is especially important when users lean across the radiator from a wheelchair to operate window controls.

U For people who take longer to react to emergencies, choose electric heat rather than gas or oil systems. Replace oil heating units with heat pumps, which offer both cooling and heating with energy efficiency.

2-19

2-20

U Heat pumps and other forced-air heating systems cause drafts, which can be problematic for people with sensation differences. Sometimes an adjustment to the airflow velocity can help. With a forced-air system, make sure the floor registers have narrow slats (not greater than 1/2 in wide)[13] and will not catch a wheelchair. (Fig. 2-21) If the register has elongated openings, place the long dimension perpendicular to the route of travel. (Fig. 2-22)

For people with hearing differences, reduce background noise and vibrations by isolating forced-air heating units in a separate room. Insulate heating and ventilation ducts to control fan noise. Replace metal duct work with 1-in insulated duct board. Silencers may also be installed near fans. Regulate airflow velocities to control turbulence-induced noise and select registers with low sound production ratings. Avoid the noise of forced-air heating systems by installing electric baseboard heating, radiant ceiling heat, or a hot water radiator. Since static may affect hearing aid operation, provide increased humidity to minimize static. An air conditioner or purifier can be added to a forced-air system or used as a separate unit. (Fig. 2-23)

U A wall heater with a fan can be used to dry off after bathing, but the grill may become hot enough to cause a burn. Specify a well-protected model than can be programmed to automatically warm the space early in the morning before use. Consider a ventilating radiant heat lamp or a ceiling heater with a fan in the dressing area for extra warmth. For people in wheelchairs, specify a fan to move the warm air to a lower level. (Fig. 2-24)

Radiant ceiling heat without a fan may not provide sufficient warmth at wheelchair height. Most of the heat stays close to the ceiling with this system. A ceiling fan will help, especially with high ceilings. The fan can be used to cool in the summer and circulate the warm air that accumulates at the top of the room in the winter. A remote control switch is available to change speeds or dim the light on the fan.

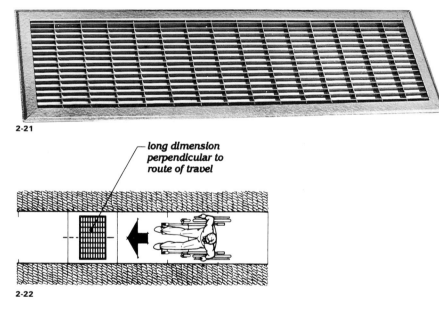

2-21

long dimension
perpendicular to
route of travel

2-22

2-23

2-24

(U) People with limited circulation may prefer a general ambient temperature of 75°F or more, while others with allergies to mold and fungi need to keep the temperature between 65 and 70°F (with relative humidity at 45 to 55 percent).[14] People with multiple sclerosis, however, are often less tolerant of heat than others. Those with cardiovascular problems are at higher risk in extremes of hot and cold, while individuals with cystic fibrosis have difficulty perspiring and are prone to heat stress. Finally, people with hyperthyroid conditions may have thermal regulation problems. In meeting these individual needs, specify a programmable heating system that allows temperatures to change over time.[15] An electronic thermostat will help conserve energy, which becomes even more important when higher ambient temperatures are required. (Fig. 2-25)

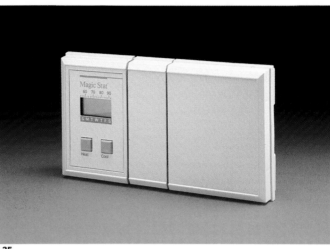

2-25

VENTILATION AND CONDITIONING

(U) Many people with thermal sensitivity problems require as many as 10 air changes per hour.[16] People with respiratory problems may prefer housing above grade on dry sites with protection from wind. A dehumidifier and air purifier may be helpful. Houseplants are also effective in purifying the air. (Fig. 2-26)

(U) For people with allergies, give extra attention to hypoallergenic heating, air purity, and ventilation. It is virtually impossible, however, to control all of the allergens in the interior. Petrochemicals, toxic finishes, adhesives, and phenols are but a few of the hundreds of irritants commonly found in building materials. In addition, common house dust, dust mites, mold spores, cigarette smoke, and animal dandruff frequently cause problems. Once the allergies have been identified, reactions can often be reduced with a combination of sensible selection of products, an uncoated paper filter system, and ventilation allowing one air change per hour. Toxins typically build up in closets and storage areas, and ventilation should be planned in these spaces as well.

Pollutant	Sources	Solutions
Formaldehyde	foam insulation plywood clothes carpeting furniture paper goods household cleaners	Philodendron Spider plant Golden pothos Bamboo palm Corn plant Chrysanthemum Mother-in-law's tongue
Benzene	tobacco smoke gasoline synthetic fibers plastics inks oils detergents rubber	English ivy Marginata Janet Craig Chrysanthemum Gerbera daisy Warneckei Peace lily
Trichloro-ethylene	dry cleaning inks paints varnishes lacquers adhesives	Gerbera Chrysanthemum Peace lily Warneckei Marginata

2-26

ACOUSTICAL DESIGN

U In health care environments, noise has been shown to contribute to more wandering by patients, less visits by family and friends, and more staff turnover.[17] Staggered stud construction is a simple idea that could be easily applied to reduce sound transmission. (Fig. 2-27). This construction technique opens an air space in the wall that can be filled with insulation. For people with allergies, avoid cellulose, fiberglass, and rock wool insulation. Specify vermiculite and perlite, which are resistant to moisture.[18] It is especially important to control sound transmission between the social and private spaces of the interior. For example, in a private residence noises from the bathroom and bedroom should be isolated from the living room.

U A variety of types of wall, floor, and ceiling finishes are available to absorb sound generated within a room. A wall of drapery, for example, can absorb nearly half of the noise produced.[19] Sound baffles used across a hallway can be effective in absorbing ambient noise while visually reducing the length of the space.

U Unwanted noise has been known to be a stress producer. It is most annoying when its source is not evident and when it is not predictable. Even if the noise cannot be eliminated, the resulting stress can be reduced or eliminated by providing a means to control the stressor.[20] In a residence, specify a tambour window treatment to control street noise. In a commercial space, spring mount transformers and isolate vibration from mechanical equipment.

U "White noise" is a mixture of frequencies used to cover distracting sounds. It has been used extensively to reduce stress. In some cases, users can control the white noise, choosing their own soothing music or tapes of running water, surf, rain, and other calming sounds. (Fig. 2-28) Although white noise can be helpful in masking unwanted sounds, it can in itself be distracting, particularly when hearing and concentration are important. When white noise is broadcast throughout a space, it can reduce orientation since it makes the area appear more uniform.[21]

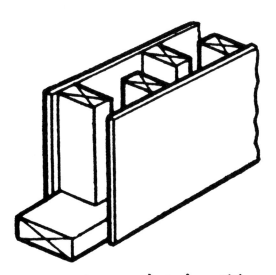

2-27 **staggered-stud partition**

2-28

SECURITY SYSTEMS

Many people with different abilities have a slower reaction time and limited strength in responding to emergencies. For these people, security systems become even more important. At least four types of systems are available: ultrasonic motion detectors, pressure mats, passive infrared photoelectric sensors, and switch sensors. Each type can be powered by batteries or direct wiring.

Ultra-high-frequency sound motion detectors in the security system can interfere with hearing aids. Use pressure mats, passive infrared photoelectric sensors, and switch sensors instead. (Fig. 2-29) (Infrared and radio frequency technology is also used for sound amplification in theaters and auditoriums to support people with hearing differences.)

For a private residence, consider an electric locking system for the entry door coupled with an intercom system. When a noise is heard, the lock can be checked by remote control from anywhere in the interior. The doorbell can be answered and the door unlocked without having to move to the entry. (Fig. 2-30) A video monitor can also be added to the system, giving a clear picture of a visitor at the front door. (Fig. 2-31) Outdoor light controls are also an essential part of this system. An entry light that comes on automatically at night is another good choice. With any electrical security system, plan a backup if power is lost.

2-29

2-30

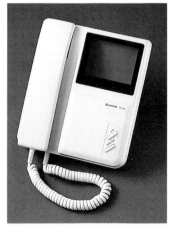

2-31

U If there is a medical emergency or security breach, proximity to the call system becomes a critical issue. Many alarm devices are available to call for help with the push of a button. One type triggers an automatic telephone communication system, which calls an answering service and plays a recorded message stating the location of the emergency. It will dial a second number if there is no answer at the first, and continues dialing both numbers until it gets a response.

U It may be important to include an emergency call system in the bathroom. Extend elastic cords through eyelets around the entire perimeter of the room at two levels, 4 in above the floor and above the door lever at 3 ft 6 in. Attach the cord to toggle switches that activate the alarm. In less critical situations, a telephone or intercom in the bathroom may be sufficient. Most intercoms can be monitored in other rooms when the channel is left open, so a call for help can be heard throughout the house. (Fig. 2-32) For a residence with young children or a client with Alzheimer's, the intercom can be used to monitor the use of outside doors. (Fig. 2-33) When a door opens, the intercom begins to beep.

U A commercial call system may be as simple as a buzzer or as involved as a teleconferencing device. A touch system could be installed on the baseboard, for example, so that a person could call for help anywhere in the building. (Fig. 2-34)

U An automatic garage door opener makes an essential contribution to security. The remote control allows people with limited strength, reach, and coordination to raise and lower the door. The garage door system should include an automatic light with at least a 15-second delay to allow time to drive into the garage. Some systems are equipped with touch pads, smoke detectors, carbon monoxide detectors, and burglar alarms for added security.

2-32

2-33

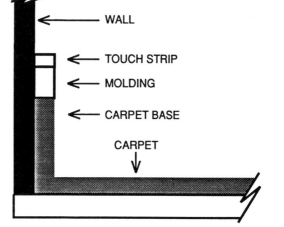

DETAIL - SIDE ELEVATION OF WALL MOUNTED TOUCH STRIP

2-34

ENVIRONMENTAL CONTROL SYSTEMS

U Remote control devices can make a significant difference in the lives of people with various abilities. Almost any switch can be changed to a remote control with a transmitter and receiver. Some transmitters are sonic and do not require a battery; others are operated by touch. Remote power door openers, for example, can be used in conjunction with bedside environmental controls to let pets in and out of the house. Even a lawn sprinkler system can be controlled from bedside. (Fig. 2-35)

U Environmental control systems operate many devices, including aide alerts, tape recorders, page turners, televisions, electric beds, lights, and drapery controls. Computer-driven systems can run security checks and lower interior temperatures when a room is not in use. (Fig. 2-36). Some systems do not require manual control but can be operated simply by puffing into the switch or controlling the switch by inhaling or "sipping." When units are operated with a puff/sip switch, tongue switch, rocking lever, communication aid, or small computer, add separate manual controls for use by a guest or aide.

U A series of tabletop rocker switches can serve as a less expensive version of an environmental control system. These units are often used to control a lamp, air conditioner, television, radio, and small intercom. The extension cords associated with this system, however, are a disadvantage.

2-35

2-36

For deaf people, consider the installation of telecommunication devices, vibrating signal system (Fig. 2-37), nonauditory door bells, closed circuit televisions, and alarms not involving audible communication. Door bells can be attached to a strobe. Also consider electrical solenoid bed vibrators, individual vibrating pagers, and variable intensity fans. For people with reduced hearing, earphones allow amplification without disturbing others. Door bells and alarms should be selected in frequencies under 10,000 Hz[22] or wired to vary the level of light in the house.

SMOKE DETECTORS

In a residence, smoke detectors should be installed adjacent to each bedroom and at the top of the stairway. Another smoke detector should be installed in the living room if it is more than 15 ft away from a bedroom unit. A third should be installed in the basement. Other possible locations include the kitchen and furnace room. Be sure to consider location in relation to air supply and air return registers. (Fig. 2-38) A gas leak detector may also be required.

Select a model with photoelectric and ion chamber detection to warn of both smoke and heat. The detector should also sound a warning when the battery needs to be replaced. Some localities allow use of a smoke detector that activates a recorder, which in turn dials the nearest police or fire department.

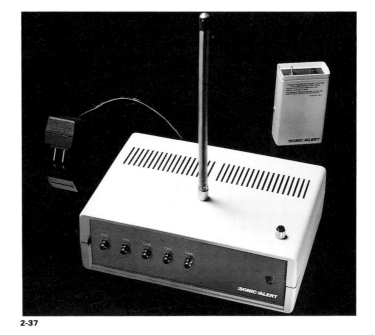

2-37

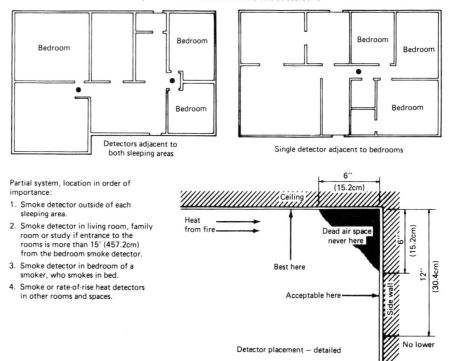

Proper locations for smoke detectors outside bedrooms

Detectors adjacent to both sleeping areas

Single detector adjacent to bedrooms

Partial system, location in order of importance:

1. Smoke detector outside of each sleeping area.
2. Smoke detector in living room, family room or study if entrance to the rooms is more than 15' (457.2cm) from the bedroom smoke detector.
3. Smoke detector in bedroom of a smoker, who smokes in bed.
4. Smoke or rate-of-rise heat detectors in other rooms and spaces.

Detector placement – detailed

Placement of smoke detectors in residential units. (*Source:* USDHUD, Gage-Babcock & Assoc. *People and Fire*, Contact H-2176R, p. 10, Washington D.C., 1977)

2-38

3. Ceiling and Wall Finishes

From color prescriptions for healing environments to the use of contrast, hue, intensity, and texture, finishes make a difference in the lives of people with different abilities. The power of design, color, and pattern can be used to turn confusion into visual organization, isolation into social integration, and monotony into stimulation.

Finishes can increase light reflectance and light quantity without increasing glare. As the eye lense yellows with age, up to 5 times more light quantity may be required for tasks. As cataracts develop, glare from this extra lighting can be incapacitating unless light-absorbing finishes are specified. Finishes can also absorb ambient noise to quiet a space for people with hearing differences or reflect sound to provide cues for people with vision differences. Skillfully used contrasting finishes can define a doorway or room perimeter, supporting the wayfinding system and efficacy of the user. The enlightened designer can make a difference through the artistic and functional use of finishes.

PATTERN AND COLOR

Pattern and color can be used to visually lower an existing ceiling. Many people in wheelchairs are more comfortable with a lower ceiling height. A lower ceiling also helps a room appear cozier and less institutional. (Fig. 3-1). Carefully choose color schemes to visually lower ceilings. Orange and red tones come to focus behind the retina of the eye and will cause the surface to visually advance or lower, while blue and green tones come to focus in front the retina and appear to recede.[1]

3-1

Yellow or blue color schemes may cause difficulties for people who have yellowing lenses. Yellow colors can become so intense that they may become annoying. Blue, blue-green, or violet color schemes may appear to be gray, especially in daylight or fluorescent light (in a blue color spectrum). Blue tones can be distinguished from other colors more easily at night when lighted by tungsten light (standard light bulbs). Red tones appear to be the least affected by vision differences.[2] Bright lighting intensifies color, while texture makes tones appear darker.[3]

Lighter color schemes that do not absorb light are important for people with vision differences. (Fig. 3-2) Dark color schemes adjacent to bright windows can "dazzle" and make it difficult for people to distinguish objects located near the window.[4]

3-2

Contrast between the floor and wall color will help people with differences in sight to distinguish the edges of a room. To evaluate this contrast, each color can be correlated to a shade of gray. If the color contrasts by more than two digits on the gray scale, there will be enough contrast to increase the imagery of objects.[5] (The gray scale consists of 10 increments from black to white and can be found illustrated on the back of many printer's rules.)

A contrasting baseboard helps to define boundaries (Fig. 3-3), and a door frame in a contrasting color will draw attention to the doorway. Since most doors are left open, the molding should contrast with the walls and match the color of the door.

There is some evidence that converging lines created by contrasting baseboard, wainscoting, valance, and handrails are perceived as a confusing pattern to people with concentration differences. This problem becomes most apparent at the end of a corridor.[6] When these elements are blended together into a monochromatic color scheme on the other hand, a hallway appears wider and shorter. This technique can visually reduce the appearance of a long institutional corridor.

A monochromatic color scheme, however, may become monotonous and boring when viewed for an extended period of time. It can contribute to sensory deprivation, which leads to disorganization of brain function, deterioration of intelligence, and an inability to concentrate. For those who suffer from a deficiency of perception, plan variety in color, pattern, and texture.

Walls of mirror, however, should not be used to add variety and expand spaces.[7] Visually confusing mirrors are too distracting and can make concentration and orientation difficult. For people who suffer from distortion of perception, keep colors and textures as unambiguous and understated as possible.[8] An interior with fewer textures and colors is also helpful for people who are susceptible to sensory overload. Low-intensity colors, especially for background surfaces, are most appropriate for this population.[9]

M People who become easily disoriented may identify with smaller spaces that are treated differently, are well defined, and are planned in human scale. Spatial definition can also help develop a sense of security. To offer a feeling of control, the perimeter walls and ceilings should be clearly defined and not extend into other spaces.

U Color can affect perceptions of time, size, weight, and volume. In a space where pleasant activities occur, such as a dining or recreation room, a warm color scheme will make the activities seem to last longer. In rooms where monotonous tasks are performed, a cool color scheme can make time pass more quickly.

U Warm color hues are often associated with extroverted responses and social contact. A quiet, relaxing, or contemplative atmosphere is created by cool hues. Cool colors can balance a warm space, whether the warmth is created with lighting, color selection, or actual temperature. Color contrast can be used to create varying moods.

U Researchers in the field of anthroposophic medicine maintain that color can be used to help patients regain health. According to their studies, color should progress from hard to soft tones as patients move from outside to inside. The most intimate and vulnerable spaces, like patient rooms, should have the softest colors. Patient rooms with warm colors are used to build up from a "cold" illness like arthritis, and cool blue or violet tones are used to dissolve or break down inflammation.[10]

U People who spend much of the day in bed may grow tired of facing a patterned or highly textured wall covering. Perforated and other ceiling patterns may also be visually confusing. Only use strong patterns on walls adjacent to or in back of the bed. Even in these locations, texture and pattern may produce a response of stimulation rather than relaxation.

Allowing clients to control the ceiling pattern can actually reduce stress. Clients may choose to project videotapes on the ceiling or suspend artwork, a technique frequently used in doctors' examination rooms.

U Stripes on the wall can appear to be bars, and wavy patterns can appear to be in motion, affecting mobility.[11] Wall coverings in small patterns and limited amounts can be pleasing to the eye. (Fig. 3-4) Primary colors like red, yellow, and blue and strong patterns are pleasing at first but may eventually become tiring. Also, the boundary between two intense colors eventually becomes visually unstable.[12] Only use intense colors for accents and for contrast to improve visual organization. Brightly colored grab bars, door frames, levers, and switches, for instance, will be easier to find.

3-4

TEXTURE

U For people who lean on a wall occasionally for support, remember that a slick, glossy wall surface offers no friction for stability. Specify well-textured patterns. (Fig. 3-5) Although a semi-gloss finish can be washed with little damage and is more resistant to soil than flat finishes, a flat finish will diffuse light, hide minor flaws, and appear less institutional. Also, shiny surfaces produce glare, which may be visually confusing.

U Heavy plaster wall texture can be damaged by wheelchairs or mobility aids. It can also be abrasive when people rub against it. For people with allergies, a light gypsum plaster on metal lath may be the best choice. It should be left unpainted, but it can be tinted with hypoallergenic, nontoxic dyes.[13] Vegetable dyes can be used in a casein and beeswax medium.[14]

C In relaxation areas, use textured sound-absorbing wall coverings that keep the space quiet. Control of ambient noise is important here to maximize concentration and hearing. (Fig. 3-6). Noise from mechanical equipment outside a room can be controlled with wall insulation. Low-frequency noise generated within the space can be absorbed by sound panels. Place the panels on at least two adjacent (not opposite) walls at the critical height for sound absorption (between 2 ft 6 in and 6 ft 8 in above the floor).[15] Be sure there are no acoustical leaks between the ceiling and the wall. (Fig. 3-7)

C Hard surfaces are often used to meet fire codes, but echoes off these surfaces can create an institutional atmosphere and cause hearing and concentration difficulties. To absorb sound, use acoustical tiles, which are fire retardant.

3-5

3-6

3-7

People with differences in vision may prefer hard, shiny surfaces and a relatively "live" sound-reflecting interior to locate sound cues.[16] (Fig. 3-8). An open doorway, for example, can be identified because it does not reflect sound like the adjacent surfaces. But in some areas, such as hallways, echoes may be confusing, making a conversation appear to be on one side of the corridor when it is really on the other.[17] Sound-absorbing finishes are a better choice in these areas.

WALL PROTECTION

Protective corners, wall coverings, moldings, and baseboards are necessary to prevent wheelchair abrasion of wall surfaces. Use 9-in-high baseboards suitable for staining for additional wall protection. Use an oil stain finish that can be touched up if scratched by wheelchair footrests. A carpet base matching the floor carpeting will minimize the institutional appearance of the high baseboard. (Fig. 3-9) Be sure that carpet base complies with local applicable fire codes.

Protect corners from wheelchair damage with recessed metal corner guards applied during construction or surface-mounted metal or plastic guards applied after construction. Clear or colored plastic guards or wood moldings are less institutional in appearance but not as durable as metal. Plastic and wood chair rails are also available. (Fig. 3-10)

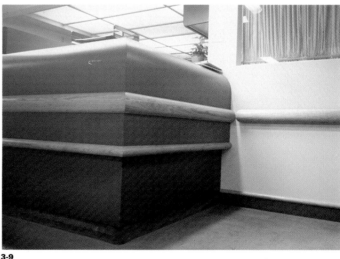

3-9

3-8

3-10

Consider low-pile, fire-retardant coordinating carpet type material on the walls of high-traffic areas for acoustical control and protection from wheelchairs. End the wall material at the height of the back of the wheelchair and cap it with a chair molding. (Fig. 3-11)

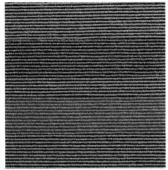

3-11

Wall carpet and fabric will significantly contribute to flame spread if inappropriately selected, but fire-retardant upholstery fabric can provide wall protection in low-traffic areas. Use a special adhesive designed for fabrics since a regular adhesive may soak through to the surface. Wall fabric can be applied directly over textured wall surfaces like concrete or over rough textures like cinder block with minimal preparation. With fabric on the wall, the space can be personalized with wall hangings without visually harming the walls; nail holes will not show when wall hangings are changed. (Fig. 3-12). Some solution-dyed polyolefin can be cleaned with undiluted chlorine bleach with no effect on the color. Fabric can also be hung, (Fig. 3-13, 3-14), using a track system, or draped over the ceiling.

3-12

3-13

3-14

Ⓤ Ceiling moldings will prevent wallpaper from peeling if they overlap the paper. They are especially necessary with heavy papers or fabrics that are used to protect walls from wheelchair or other abrasions.

Ⓤ Vinyl wall covering weighing at least 13 oz per square yard can also offer abrasion resistance.[18] It is especially useful in areas where spills are a problem. Tedlar and Prefixx are both nonporous and prevent stains from migrating into the vinyl.[19] They are more expensive than some wall fabrics, show nail holes more easily, and do not offer the acoustical absorption qualities of fabric. Still, they can be lined to cushion a wall from wheelchair contact and offer some acoustical control of low-frequency noise.

Ⓤ A chair rail is an important addition to dining or conference areas where chairs are used with delicate wall finishes. It can also protect the wall from wheelchair abrasion. Wainscoting can serve the same purpose, but it will visually reduce the size of a small room. (Fig. 3-15)

Ⓤ Textured tongue-and-groove planking in an oil finish is a good choice for walls exposed to abrasion. (Fig. 3-16) It should be glued and nailed to the wall before the finish is applied. An oil finish can be easily repaired if damaged by wheelchair abrasion. Thin wood paneling has a higher flame spread rating than planking. Heat causes delamination and separation of the paneling, allowing the wood to burn more easily. Prefabricated scored paneling has an institutional appearance and cannot be easily touched up if scratched.

◖ Wood veneer rolls can be applied like wallpaper at a lower cost than solid wood. Veneers can also be wrapped around curved surfaces. Tambour wood sheets will also serve this purpose and offer additional wall protection. In barrier-free design, curved corners are often specified to increase the view around the corner and prevent accidents. (Fig. 3-17)

3-15

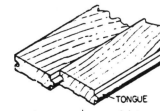

tongue-and-groove joint

3-16

3-17

Ⓤ Specify stains on frames and doors whenever possible; limit the use of paint and varnish, which are more difficult to touch up. With abrasion caused by wheelchairs, crutches, or leg braces, oil-base stains can be sanded and touched up in spots without major refinishing. When specifying resin or paint, use an epoxy surface wall paint with a water-resistant finish to prevent the paint from washing off. Urethane resin paints are so tough they are often used for floors, but they are not as resistant to fading as epoxy. (Fig. 3-18)

Ⓤ Ceramic wall tile offers excellent protection from wheelchair abrasion as well as water damage. It can be easily maintained if a colored latex cement grout is specified. Darker grouts are not as easily stained, and latex additives to portland cement will make grout less absorptive. Silicone and urethane grouts also resist stains on walls.[20] Wall tile should be installed in portland cement when moisture and pressure are present.

EVALUATION GUIDE: PAINTS

Property	Resin					
	oil	alkyd	epoxy	urethane	vinyl	acrylic
Abrasion Resistance	2	3	4	5	3	4
Hardness	2	3	4	5	3	4
Flexibility	3	3	5	4	5	5
Adhesion	4	4	5	3	3	5
Resistance to:						
Acid	1	2	5	5	3	3
Alkali	1	2	5	4	3	4
Detergent	2	2	5	4	3	3
Fading	3	4	3	2	5	5
Heat	2	3	3	3	3	4
Moisture	3	3	4	4	2	2
Strong Solvents	1	2	5	5	3	3

3-18

Legend:
5 = excellent
4 = very good
3 = good
2 = fair
1 = poor

4. Windows and Doors

Perhaps more than any other products, improperly specified windows and doors have caused problems for people with differences in ability. A door may be either too wide and heavy to open or too narrow for wheelchair passage. A door closer, added for people in wheelchairs, may require too much strength to open. A vision panel in the door, so helpful in preventing accidents, may produce too much glare for people with differences in vision.

It is obvious that specialized knowledge is required to meet the varied needs of this population. Training is particularly critical in the area of window and door specification, where mistakes are easily made and expensive to correct.

WINDOWS

Window Types

Both the design of the window and the location of the controls can improve wheelchair access. Casement, sliding, hopper, or awning windows with controls on the bottom are easier to reach from a wheelchair. Make sure latches can be operated with a closed fist and corners of sills are rounded to prevent injury. Double-hung windows can drop unintentionally, are difficult for everyone to open, and are often too high to be reached from a wheelchair. Although emergency exit is not possible through an awning window, this design is easier to reach and open than a double-hung installation. (Fig. 4-1) An awning window can be installed inside an open double-hung window.

4-1

43

4-2

4-3

⬤ Many crank-type casement windows are easier to use than sliders, although a slider with ball bearings may also be easy to operate. A longer crank or lever arm multiplies the force. Place levers so that they can be operated with the strongest hand for greater power. Casement windows with levers or push rods do not require as large a range of motion as do horizontal sliders or pivoting sashes. Casement windows and horizontal pivot sashes are also easier to clean. The window lock should be installed within reach from a wheelchair. (Fig. 4-2)

⬛ A sliding window panel or shutter on a track may be easier to operate from a wheelchair than a hinged panel. (Fig. 4-3) The top panel of a double-hung shutter is often higher than 4 ft and not reachable from a wheelchair. For safety, choose windows and shutters that won't drop unintentionally or swing in the wind.

⬤ People with limited circulation often need higher ambient temperatures, and people in wheelchairs must operate in the lower, often colder, part of a room. For these clients, heat loss and solar gain become critical issues. Reduce the header or window height and create an overhang to reduce solar gain. Double-glazed sliding windows conserve energy but may be too heavy for many people to operate. For people with strength limits, specify double-glazed push-button windows. These typically have a vertical control to adjust the window opening and are manually operated. They are preferable to windows with power drive, which cannot be used during a power failure.

⬤ Many people with different abilities have an increased need for security. Consider using bay or bow windows, which offer a more complete view of the surroundings. They also allow more light into a room. (Fig. 4.4)

4-4

U Glass windows can be more easily broken than plastic but will not provide intruder protection. For people who are autistic or prone to seizures or falls, use tempered glass or plastic in low-level windows. Wired glass can also be used but has a more institutional appearance. Heavy-duty plastic windows with locking devices are strong and resistant to force. Locate the lock as far away from the glass or plastic as possible. Look for windows with pins that insert into the frame to prevent the window from opening even if the lock has been breached.

4-5

Window Treatments

Both the type of window treatments and the location of the installation need to be considered for wheelchair access. Treatments mounted within the window frame block some of the light and view but free extra wall space for storage within reach. (Fig. 4-5) Stacking drapery outside of the frame on the wall adjacent to the window requires approximately one-third of the window width in wall space to clear the window.

For people who are susceptible to glare, choose sheer window treatments to allow diffused sunlight into the space. Direct sunlight may "dazzle" and cause temporary blindness. (Fig. 4-6)

4-6

Many window treatments that insulate the space from temperature changes will also insulate the interior from exterior noise. Consider heavy draperies with a separate liner (Fig. 4-7) or heavy roman shades that seal around the perimeter of the window. These soft surfaces also absorb the ambient noise generated within the room while preventing noise from being transmitted from the outside.

U Make sure cords on roller shades and wands on blinds are long enough to reach from a wheelchair. Wall-mount cords on blinds and draperies to keep them handy and within reach. Add beads to wall-mounted cords to improve grip strength. Do not mount cords over counters where they would be difficult to reach. Corners over counters are particularly difficult.

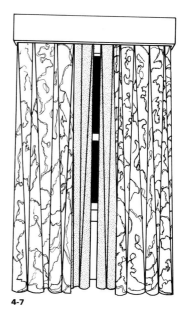

4-7

4-8

4-9

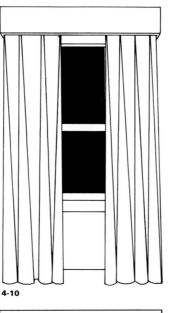

4-10

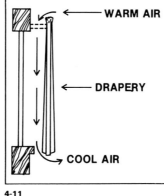

WARM AIR

DRAPERY

COOL AIR

4-11

For people with limited manual dexterity, consider electric drapery rod controls or wall-mounted drapery cords. Wands on blinds and shades can also be operated electrically by switch or remote control. Remember that any electrical device will require additional maintenance. (Fig. 4-8)

Many people with different abilities require extra time to respond to a fire. Flame-retardant fabrics are a logical choice for window treatments. Modacrylic or fire-resistant polyester fabrics drape well but cannot be laundered in hot water. Polyester has the added disadvantages of pilling, staining, and collecting static electricity. Although fiberglass is flameproof, it does not drape well and can cause skin irritations.

For people who spend some daylight hours in bed, use a reflective blackout lining to darken the room for sleeping. It will reflect heat during the day and serve as a barrier to both air and moisture while protecting draperies from sun damage.

Reduce high heating and cooling costs with the right choices in window treatments. Exterior shades or awnings give the most effective protection from extremes in heat. (Fig. 4-9) Draperies, on the other hand, transfer less heat to the room than interior blinds or shades.[1]

Insulating draperies must be installed within $1/2$ in of the floor and ceiling or protected by a cornice for good thermal control. (Fig. 4-10) Heat rises behind shorter draperies, causing convection currents that actually cool the space in winter (Fig. 4-11) and heat it in summer.

Drapery accessories can also improve energy efficiency. For example, draperies can be sealed to the wall with tacks, magnetic tape, Velcro, or moldings to reduce heat loss and gain. With fabrics that adhere to Velcro, the overlap in the center can be sealed with a Velcro strip that is hidden from view. Light-colored linings reflect solar energy and keep rooms cooler, while darker colors absorb the heat.

Ⓤ Insulated shades are available that seal the window for maximum control. They completely block out light and view, however, and are not appropriate for daytime light control. Solar shades allow light and view but are not as effective as shades that seal.

Ⓤ Specify shades that overlap the window on all sides to minimize heat and light leaks. Existing inside-mounted shades and draperies can be covered with a lambrequin, which controls light leaks and offers thermal protection. (Fig. 4-12)

Ⓤ Many people with different abilities have very limited time and energy, and window maintenance becomes a critical factor. Draperies require a special heading to be machine washable. A washable snap-tape system can be used so that drapery pins will not have to be removed and replaced. (Fig. 4-13) Vertical louvers on shutters and blinds are easy to maintain. Horizontal louvers may be dust traps and cause problems for people with allergies unless they are installed between panes of thermal glass. With fabric-filled shutters, fabric should be removable for maintenance. Fabric on padded cornices can be installed with snap tape or Velcro for easy removal and cleaning.

4-12

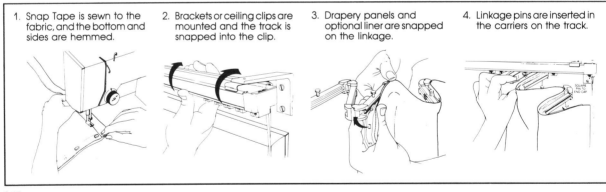

1. Snap Tape is sewn to the fabric, and the bottom and sides are hemmed.
2. Brackets or ceiling clips are mounted and the track is snapped into the clip.
3. Drapery panels and optional liner are snapped on the linkage.
4. Linkage pins are inserted in the carriers on the track.

4-13

DOORS

Doors Types

 Eliminate the vertical strip between double doors, since it is often not detected by blind people who use canes. Doors that open at an angle into high-traffic areas may also be hazardous. Plan sliding interior doors to eliminate this problem. Pocket doors often solve space-planning problems, but the hardware is difficult for many to use. (Fig. 4-14) The hardware can be replaced with a grooved bar if a lock is not necessary. Dutch doors are also a problem since the top half of double-hung doors often cannot be detected by a blind person using a cane.

M People who are hesitant to socialize with a group may prefer the partial privacy of a double-hung door. With the bottom half of the door closed, they can listen in before actually entering a room.

To operate swinging doors, people in wheelchairs must often reach, grasp, pull, back up, turn, and go around. Sliding interior doors that stack out of the way are the best choices for wheelchair access. Folding doors also work well, but it is easy for children and others to pinch their fingers in these doors. If these doors are on a track, make sure the track is recessed and is not an obstacle for entry. Accordion folding doors or a drapery will also work.

U Sliding top-hung doors with bottom guides may be easier to move than those that slide on a bottom track. Choose nylon wheels or roller bearings with self-lubricating metal tracks.

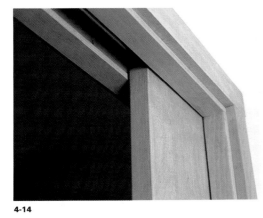

4-14

4-15

4-16

French doors are often specified for wheelchair access, but unless each door is wider than 32 in, both must be opened. From a wheelchair, it may be difficult to open both doors at the same time. (Fig. 4-15) Unless narrow interior French doors can be left permanently open, replace them with folding doors or a single sliding door.

Solid core doors require more strength to open and close than hollow core doors. Doors should be kept to a minimum width to keep them lighter and easier to open. Sliding glass exterior doors can be very difficult to operate because of the width and weight of each door. Also, the accumulation of dirt in the door track can render the doors inoperable. Consider a hinged glass door as a replacement. For people who are autistic or prone to seizures and falls, use tempered glass. Glass doors should be protected from wheelchair abrasion by a bottom rail.

To measure the force necessary to open a door, attach a spring scale to it, then open the door slowly and evenly. Many people cannot open exterior doors that require more than 8.5 pounds of force (lbf). Interior doors and all sliding doors should require less than 5 lbf.[2]

Doors that stick or drag require needless effort. The problem can often be corrected by oiling the hinges or removing the old paint on the edges of the doors. If this does not work, remove the door, plane and sand the edges, shim the hinges, or rehang the door on new hardware. For people with coordination limits, sand leading edges of doors to eliminate a sharp edge and minimize possible injury. Specify an oil finish for easy touch-up. For people with allergies, use a water-base sealant or a hard finish polyurethane.[3]

Doors can be selected to reduce transmitted noise and improve hearing ability within the space. Make sure all door and wall assemblies eliminate acoustical leaks. Inspect gaskets and use laminated or double-glazed glass in doors and windows. (Fig. 4-16)

In commercial spaces, specify alternative doors or gates adjacent to revolving doors and turnstiles. Some doors require an extra panel that can be opened when wider access is necessary.

For people who must spend part of the day in bed, use French or atrium patio doors in a wide width that allow the bed to be moved outdoors. Wider doors also allow the addition of large pieces of furniture to the room. (Fig. 4-17)

For security purposes, the best protection is a metal door and frame. With existing sliding glass doors, add screws to the top to prevent doors from being lifted out of the frame. Wooden entry door frames (even with a dead bolt) can be forced with a well-placed kick.

4-17

Door Hardware and Accessories

Door accessories for wheelchair use include levers, door closers, thresholds, protective plates, vision panels, and hinges. Doors should be equipped with double-action hinges so they can swing both ways. Be sure the action of the door does not interfere with foot traffic.

If the door is too narrow for wheelchair use, try removing the doorstop for an added amount of clearance. Offset pivot hinges will increase the width of the open doorway by an additional 2 in. This may be all that is required for the necessary 32-in clear opening.[4] Whenever possible, specify 34 in of clear space. (Fig. 4-18)

For people who are autistic or prone to seizures, use rising pin-butt hinges for easy door removal in case of seizure behind a locked door, or be sure interior locks can be opened with a screwdriver. (Fig. 4-19) This is especially important on the bathroom door.

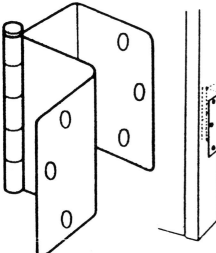

Designed for Barrier-Free Life   **"Adds Two Inches To Any Doorway"**

4-18

4-19

4-20

U A rising pin-butt hinge can also be used to elevate weather stripping from floor surfaces. Maneuvering over interior thresholds may be difficult for people in wheelchairs. Thresholds often serve no purpose and should be removed. Exterior thresholds should be no higher than 1/2 in; avoid sliding glass doors because many require higher thresholds. Bevel thresholds to a vertical slope no greater than 1:2.[5] (Fig. 4-20) To totally eliminate the threshold on swinging doors, use movable mortise-type weather stripping, which will lower to the floor when the door is closed. (Fig. 4-21)

U On the exterior door, add a mail slot at latch height. (Fig. 4-22) Before installing the slot, make sure the post office will agree to deliver mail to the door. Attach an insulated box on the interior side of the door to catch the mail and prevent heat loss or gain. A larger insulated box could be used to keep delivered meals at the proper temperature.

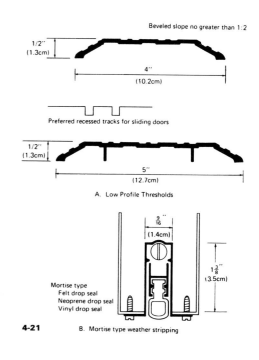

Beveled slope no greater than 1:2

1/2″ (1.3cm)

4″ (10.2cm)

Preferred recessed tracks for sliding doors

1/2″ (1.3cm)

5″ (12.7cm)

A. Low Profile Thresholds

9/16″ (1.4cm)

1 3/8″ (3.5cm)

Mortise type
Felt drop seal
Neoprene drop seal
Vinyl drop seal

4-21   B. Mortise type weather stripping

915

On an exterior door, add a peephole at eye level from a wheelchair (between 3 ft 6 in and 4 ft).[6] For visitors in wheelchairs, lower the door knocker to the same height and consider attaching cords to the door levers to allow the door to be pulled closed more easily.

A pneumatic door closer can offer convenience for people in wheelchairs who have the strength to operate it. It is also useful for people with vision limits because a door left open at an angle into a traffic area may present an unexpected problem. A delayed-action door closer will help to keep the exterior door from blowing closed during use. (Fig. 4-23) Make sure the closer will allow the door to remain open to a full 90° for 20 seconds to allow wheelchair passage.[7] If not, substitute a lightweight spring device. Rising pin-butts are not sufficiently reliable as door closers.

To close the door without a door closer, add a C grip handle mounted on the hinge side of the door. Again, this requires strength to use, but it does offer convenience. (Fig. 4-24) Another manual system for difficult doors is a pulley-operated door opener and closer.

For people in wheelchairs or people with strength limits, use a power door opener activated by a remote control, a floor mat sensor, a wall switch, or a photo cell. (Fig. 4-25) One model even closes the door when it gets wet. An accessory is available to stop the door if it meets an object during closing. Make sure automatic sliding doors have a "break out" feature in case of power failure. Force required should be no more than 15 lbf.[8]

4-23

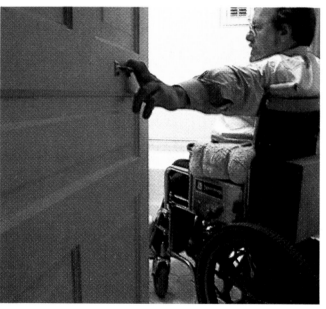

4-24

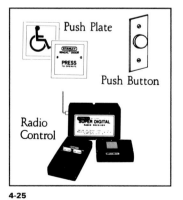

4-25

People with vision limits are often injured by swinging power doors or sliding doors with malfunctioning motion detectors. Air curtains and manually operated doors are better choices. Texture on the door lever or pull will warn that the door leads to a dangerous area, such as a loading dock, boiler room, stage, or electrical equipment room. The texture can be made by knurling or by applying a carborundum-epoxy–coated abrasive surface to the lever.[9] Do not use texture on the emergency exit door hardware, even if the door leads to a stairway. Exterior thresholds should be color contrasted; interior thresholds should be eliminated.

Limit the height of a doormat to 1/4 in and secure it to the floor with beveled metal trim or tape. A recessed carpet mat should not exceed 1/2 in in pile height.[10] A recessed grating doormat in the floor of the entryway is more stable than a moveable mat, especially for people who use electric wheelchairs. (Fig. 4-26)

To protect doors from abrasion, consider a high kick plate (16 in) on manually operated doors. Extend the plate the full width of the door on the push side. The corners of metal plates should be filed or bent toward the door to avoid possible injury. A clear acrylic door guard scratches more easily than metal but is less institutional in appearance. A plate is preferable to projecting rails, which could catch a wheelchair.

4-26

U A metal bar or decal over a sliding glass door makes the door more visible and can prevent accidents. [For security purposes, a bar can also be used to block a sliding glass door.]

U Vision panels in doors (with the bottom of the panels no higher than 3 ft) allow a person in a wheelchair to see and be seen. On an exterior door, a vision panel helps to monitor visitors. (Fig. 4-27) On an interior door, the panel lets the person become oriented to ongoing activities before entering a room. Be aware that people with vision limits can mistake panels that extend to the floor for door openings.

U Levers (mounted at a height of 30 in)[11] on both interior and exterior doors are convenient for people in wheelchairs, children, and others with strength limits. They are much easier to use from a seated position than doorknobs. Horizontal levers require less operating force than vertical levers. (Fig. 4-28) Levers should turn toward door hinges for easier access. They should have a slight return to keep them from catching on clothing. (Fig. 4-29)

4-27

4-28

4-29

4-30

U Use extra-length doorstops to protect walls from door levers. Choose an extra-length doorstop that doubles as a hook for clothes. (Fig. 4-30) To protect walls from doorknobs, use doorstops mounted to the door hinges, or wall-mount spring-loaded stops. It is easy to trip over a floor-mounted doorstop.

U Paddles on doors can be specified if they can be easily maneuvered with one hand. Avoid doorknobs; never specify a knob on one side of the set and a lever on the other, because the spring of the lever is too strong for the knob. Avoid hardware requiring simultaneous two-handed operation. An example would be a lock requiring the user to turn the key with one hand and pull with the other. Specify a pushbutton system which can be opened with one hand. If a dead bolt is used, specify a set that will disengage both the dead bolt and the door latch with one motion. For people who don't have the strength to operate the dead bolt, a slide bolt will provide nearly the same amount of security and is easier to handle.

4-31

U Doors without latches should have a C grip on the pull side and a push bar on the push side. Doors with C grips on both sides give the misleading message that both sides should be pulled. Avoid doors with knobs installed in the center of the door. These often require more strength to operate and are confusing, since it is difficult to determine which way the door will swing.

U If young children or people with orientation limits are present, use a quick-release combination lock on doors to potentially dangerous areas, such as the head of a stairway or the entrance to a furnace room. (Fig. 4-31)

5. Floor Covering

A single type of floor covering is often specified throughout the interior to add continuity to the design, but the monotony can make orientation more difficult. If a person has difficulty in keeping his or her head in an upright position, he or she may take visual cues from lower levels, including floor covering. A variety of colors and patterns can help the individual delineate different spaces.

Wheeling across carpeting requires more effort than wheeling across a hard-surfaced floor, but carpeting offers several advantages. First, it offers value as an insulator and is especially appreciated by children or people in health care facilities because it feels so much warmer on bare feet. Second, it is more comfortable for people who like to spend some time out of the wheelchair on the floor. Finally, it absorbs noise, thus keeping the interior quieter.

Studies show that carpeting can reduce ambient noise by up to 70 percent.[1] It also prevents generation of surface noise and reduces impact noise transmitted from floor to floor. Even noise from mechanical equipment can be significantly reduced by carpeting when used with floor insulation and padding. Cut pile absorbs more sound than loop pile.[2]

Ceramic tile, wood, rubber, and vinyl floor coverings are all appropriate for wheelchair users but are not always the safest choice for ambulatory clients. Vinyl or wood floors may require a nonskid polish. Surprisingly, research has revealed that hard-surfaced floors are not safer than carpet for controlling fungal or bacterial growth.[3]

CARPET

Carpet Construction

Evaluate carpets for resistance to static, flame, mildew, abrasion, fading, and permanent staining, as well as for resiliency. A resilient carpet is especially important for wheelchair use. (Fig. 5-1) Although nylon 6,6 is slightly less resistant to stains and fading than the polypropylene (olefin) fiber, it equals or exceeds olefin in every other area, especially in resiliency, dying flexibility, styling versatility, appearance, and "hand" or feel of the carpet. (Fig. 5-2)

EVALUATION GUIDE: PERFORMANCE CHARACTERISTICS OF CARPET FIBERS

Property	Fiber					
	Nylon 6,6	Nylon 6	Acryl	Olefin	Poly	Wool
HEALTH & SAFETY						
Flame Resistance	4	3	1	3	2	3
Static Resistance	3	3	3	3	3	2
Mildew Resistance	3	3	3	3	3	1
WEAR LIFE Durability						
Abrasion Resistance	4	4	2	3	2	2
Appearance Retention						
Resiliency	4	3	3	1	2	3
Soil Resistance	4	4	2	4	2	3
Stain Resistance	3	3	2	4	3	2
Fade Resistance	3	1	3	4	3	3
Maintenance						
Cleanability	4	4	2	4	2	3
ENVIRONMENTAL						
Dying Flexibility	4	4	3	2	2	3
Styling Versatility	4	4	2	2	2	3

Legend:
Poly = polyester
4 = excellent
3 = good
2 = fair
1 = poor

5-1

5-2

The face weight (also called pile weight) of a carpet refers to the amount of yarn in a given area. In considering carpets of the same face weight and fiber, a lower pile and higher tuft density give the best performance. An increase in face weight will increase performance to a maximum of 30 oz per sq yd in loop and 40 oz per sq yd in cut.[4] Increased face weight also increases the sound absorption properties, but a corresponding increase in pile height can make the carpet more difficult for wheelchair use. (Fig. 5-3)

Carpet used with wheelchairs should not exceed ½-in pile height; ¼-in height may be necessary for people with differences in strength. (Fig. 5-4) Use an uncut or tip sheer in a high-density pile for an easy traverse. Cut pile may pull the wheelchair in the direction of the nap.

A single-level loop pile wears best, but unless it is carefully selected, it can appear institutional. (Fig. 5-5) Multi-level loops and random sheer pile offer more texture, which tends to hide seams and soil. Cut pile has the shortest wear life, but is the most residential in appearance. A frieze or highly twisted pile has the best appearance retention of the cut piles. A tightly twisted ply of crimped fibers in an uncut loop construction is the most resilient for wheelchair use. (Fig. 5-6)

PROPERTIES AFFECTED BY THE STRUCTURE OF CARPET

Property Affected	Tuft Density	Face Weight	Tuft Type	Face Fiber	Color	Dye Method	Texture Pattern
WEAR LIFE Durability							
Abrasion Res.	X	X	X	X			
Appearance Retention							
Resilience	X	X	X	X			
Soil Hiding				X	X		X
Color Change			X	X	X	X	
Maintenance							
Cleanability	X		X	X	X	X	X
ENVIRONMENTAL							
Acoustics	X	X	X				
Comfort	X	X					
Ambience	X	X	X		X		X
Wheeled Equip.	X	X	X				

5-3

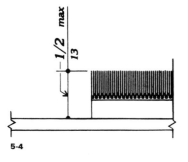

5-4

5-5

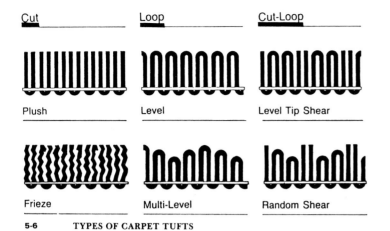

Cut

Loop

Cut-Loop

Plush

Level

Level Tip Shear

Frieze

Multi-Level

Random Shear

5-6   TYPES OF CARPET TUFTS

Carpet reduces the incidence of falls and cushions any falls that do occur. The carpet should have a pile height of $1/4$ to $1/2$ in, and the pile should be of a high density. A carpet surface that is too soft is easy to sink into and may cause loss of balance. Large loops can catch on braces, canes, and walkers.

Choose a carpet with an added biological guard to prevent bacteria growth and resulting odors. Make sure this carpet has been treated for stain resistance, and do not install it in areas with intense sunlight. The Centers for Disease Control rate carpet as safe as hard-surfaced flooring in control of bacteria and fungi if maintained properly.[5] For people with dust allergies, however, hard-surface flooring is a better choice than carpeting, which can harbor dust and dust mites.

For people who have coordination differences, consider needle-punched polypropylene (olefin) or nylon textured flooring with vinyl backing. (Fig. 5-7) These choices combine the feel and appearance of carpet with the one-step cleaning of resilient flooring, a real advantage if accidents or incontinence are problems. Since the carpet fibers are imbedded directly into the backing, the result is increased tuft bind, decreased edge ravel, and moisture-proof seams. People with incontinence may associate cold, hard floors with going to the bathroom and would appreciate carpet in lower maintenance areas.

Olefin polypropylene can be cleaned easily, will not retain odors, and is more comfortable and safer than hard-surfaced flooring. It has a low melting point, however, and can show scorch marks from the friction generated when furniture is dragged over it too rapidly. It is less resilient than other fibers, especially with wheelchair use.

5-7

Choose synthetic primary carpet backings for areas with spills, such as bathrooms and dining rooms. Spun-bonded olefin is a good choice for the primary backing. It keeps spills on the surface of the carpet for easier cleaning while preventing rot, mildew, and shrinkage. Some people prefer carpeting in the bathroom for comfort and to cushion falls. If it is installed over a hard-surfaced floor covering using double-faced tape, the carpet can be removed easily for cleaning.

Use a woven primary and secondary back, such as stainless jute, for a stretched installation in areas where moisture is not a factor. Woven backs are an excellent choice for an installation requiring good tuft bind (with children pulling at the carpet tufts, for example). Some solid primary and secondary backs are also designed for this purpose. Woven and felted carpets provide excellent tuft bind.

A carpet with a woven secondary back, like jute, can also be easily glued to a dry subfloor (without a cushion). For a softer surface, foam rubber–backed carpets glue down well, but they are very difficult to take up for replacement.

For people with hearing differences, reduce electrical interference with hearing aids by installing static-resistant carpeting throughout the interior. Existing carpet can also be treated to prevent static.

5-8

Carpet Installation

Do not glue down carpet over building expansion joints. Ask the installer for a plan of seam locations. Make sure seams are not located in high-traffic areas. Generally, do not choose the less permanent "release adhesives" even though they make the carpet easier to replace. For a releasable bond, specify a carpet that incorporates its own adhesive system. These systems can be rapidly installed, reducing the downtime on commercial projects.

Specifications should instruct the installer to save the scraps; they can be used to replace burns and stains at a later date. This is especially important when designing for people with coordination differences. Specify that the installer should remove all doors before installing, and should be sure that the subfloor is clean and free of wax before gluing. Instruct the installer to maintain a consistent pile direction.

For people with incontinence, seal concrete slabs with an acrylic polymer before installing carpeting. If the concrete flooring is hydrophilic, it will absorb liquids and their odors as it expands and contracts.[6]

Area rugs should be permanently installed for wheelchair access. The small wheels of standard wheelchairs may cause the area rug to gather in front of the user. People in electric wheelchairs may also be immobilized, and the rug may become tangled with the mechanism. Use area rugs only in low-traffic areas to personalize sections of a large room or to draw attention to specific pieces of furniture.

You can create the look of an area rug by using wall-to-wall carpeting with an inset in a contrasting color or pattern. (Fig. 5-8) Borders can be used to blend carpet colors between rooms, but keep the contrast to a minimum so that a border is not mistaken for a step. Carpeting can also be inset in tile without a change in level. (Fig. 5-9)

It is often difficult to spot a slight elevation in floor level. Single steps, thresholds, carpet strips (especially across hallways), and the edges of area rugs all present a tripping hazard. Use a bevel when changing from one floor surface to another if the change is between $1/4$ and $1/2$ in. (Fig. 5-10) Use a small ramp if the change exceeds $1/2$ in.

Avoid metal carpet strips between rooms as they may pose a tripping hazard. Instead, sew carpets together at doorways, or use graduated carpet strips. (Fig. 5-11)

5-9

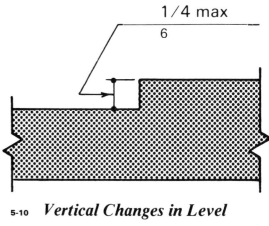

5-10 *Vertical Changes in Level*

5-11

Carpet Underlayment

Padding adds comfort for people in wheelchairs who spend time on the floor out of the wheelchair, even though it makes wheeling more difficult. If a pad is used, specify a hair pad that is firm and resilient, resisting crushing by the wheelchair. It may be easier to negotiate from a wheelchair if latex rubber is applied to both sides of the pad.

A pre-applied adhesive system also works well. The carpet and pad are glued directly to the floor. (Fig. 5-12) The pad reduces rippling and minimizes drag on the wheelchair if a thin, dense style is specified.

For the easiest wheelchair ride over the carpet and for a more stable surface offering sure footing, eliminate padding on the carpet installation. A glue-down installation also prevents rippling caused by wheelchair use.

Padding is responsible for many odor problems. If a pad is necessary for comfort or acoustics, choose a solid synthetic style sealed to prevent absorption. Do not use a fibrous, waffle, or composite construction or a rubber pad, which can rot.

Carpet Pattern

For people with differences in vision, avoid patterned and sculptured carpeting, which can make small objects on the surface difficult to locate. Contrast the carpet with the wall color to highlight the edges of the room. Also choose a carpet that contrasts with the furniture to prevent collisions. (Fig. 5-13)

Limit the contrast between carpets, however, since transitions and wide stripes can be perceived as a change in elevation. A carpet with high-contrast patterns may also be perceived as a variation in floor height. Use subtle patterns in lighter colors, which increase light quantity throughout the space without increasing glare.

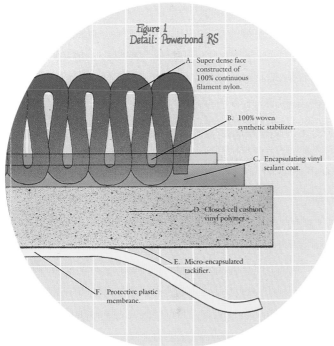

Figure 1
Detail: Powerbond RS

A. Super dense face constructed of 100% continuous filament nylon.

B. 100% woven synthetic stabilizer.

C. Encapsulating vinyl sealant coat.

D. Closed-cell cushion vinyl polymer.

E. Micro-encapsulated tackifier.

F. Protective plastic membrane.

5-12

5-13

WOOD FLOORS

Textured wood floors in some oiled finishes offer surprisingly good traction and do not require polishing. Avoid wood floors with polyurethane finishes, which offer limited traction. They are especially difficult for people in electric wheelchairs.

A tongue-and-groove construction is available in many woods and is a necessity for a stable installation on a poor subfloor. Use an oil finish on hardwood in low-traffic areas subject to scratching (e.g., under chairs); it can be touched up more easily than resin finishes. Use synthetic finishes in high-traffic areas. Acrylic-impregnated processes can be safely treated with gamma radiation to harden surfaces and prevent dents and chips. These surfaces never need waxing or protective coating and are the only wood floors that are appropriate in high-traffic areas. The acrylic saturation process also helps improve flame spread ratings and resistance to bacterial growth. The textured acrylic finishes offer better traction than polyurethane. (Fig. 5-14)

VINYL FLOORS

Solid vinyl floors with a nonskid polish are a good choice for wheelchair use. Cushioned vinyl floors require slightly more effort to use with a wheelchair than solid vinyl surfaces. Install vinyl to cover up the wall beneath wheel-in counters and to protect the kick space. (Fig. 5-15)

Sheet goods prevent leakage from spills and protect the subfloor better than vinyl tiles, especially if the seams are chemically or heat welded. Leakage in the seams promotes bacterial growth; a seamless installation is therefore important for people with allergies. Adhesives and leveling compounds should be avoided. Monolithic high-density vinyl floor coverings are acceptable to most people with allergies if fastened with wood baseboards.[7]

5-14

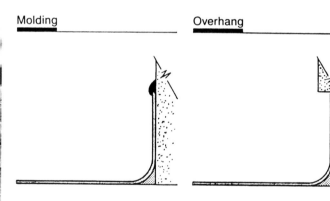

TERMINATION OF FLASH COVING
5-15

Ⓤ Floors with a large percentage of vinyl resin are the most resistant to stains. (Fig. 5-16) Solid colors will appear to be soiled more quickly than patterned floors. Soiling is also exaggerated by very light or dark colors.

Ⓤ Cushioned floors can be permanently dented by braces, canes, high heels, or other sharp objects, but they do reduce such high-frequency noises as footsteps. They are not durable enough to be used in high-traffic situations, however. Rubber and solid vinyl floors are the most resilient and dent resistant.

Ⓤ Self-shining synthetics will eventually need touch-up and should not be used in high-traffic areas. Solid vinyl floors or floors with a large proportion of vinyl resins are the best choice for abrasion resistance in such areas. Solid-colored vinyls or inlaid patterns are more resistant to abrasion than vinyl prints or rubber. Inlaid stripes are often used for wayfinding in commercial spaces. Low-voltage lighting strips can also be inserted in floor covering to aid in wayfinding.

EVALUATION GUIDE: RESILIENT FLOORINGS

This table compares resilient floorings with one another. It does not compare the properties of resilient floorings with those of carpet or hard surface floorings.

Property	Types of Resilient Floorings				
	Vinyl Backed	Vinyl Solid	Vinyl Comp	Asphalt	Rubber
HEALTH & SAFETY					
Slip Resistance	2*	2*	1*	1*	3*
WEAR LIFE					
Durability					
Abrasion Resistance	4	4	3	1	3
Appearance Retention					
Resilience	3	4	2	1	4
Static Load Resistance	2	3	2	1	4
Moisture Resistance	4	4	3	2	4
Chemical Resistance					
Acids and Alkalis	4	4	3	3	2
Oil and Grease	4	4	3	1	2
Cigarette Burn Resistance	1	1	2	1	4
Maintenance					
Ease of Maintenance	3	3	2	1	4
ENVIRONMENTAL					
Comfort Underfoot	2	4	2	1	4
Sound Absorption	2	3	2	1	4
INSTALLATION					
Ease of Installation#	3,4	3,4	4	2	3,4
Flexibility	3	4	2	1	4
Cost	High	High	Medium	Low	High

* Varies considerably according to surface finish or polish.
# Tiles of any given material are easier to install than sheet goods.

Legend:
4 = Excellent
3 = Very Good
2 = Good
1 = Fair

5-16

In bathrooms or other potentially slippery areas, specify sheet vinyl impregnated with corundum chips. The seams can be chemically or heat welded to prevent leakage. This surface is easier to maintain than some other nonslip floors.

RUBBER FLOORS

Self-shining synthetics may be too slick for many people. Rubber and vinyl floors offer better traction and are often self-waxing, requiring only occasional maintenance with a commercial buffer.

5-17

Rubber flooring shows fewer scuff marks than solid vinyl. (Fig. 5-17) It is resistant to wear, slippage, abrasion, cigarette burns, and most oils, acids, and alkalis. Rubber surfaces are not recommended for commercial kitchens, operating rooms, or spaces subject to heavy rolling loads.[8] Patterned vinyl can be substituted since it resists grease and oil and does not easily show scuff marks.

A rubber floor polished with a water emulsion offers better traction for wheelchairs than does a smooth quarry tile. It is a good choice for slip resistance in the bathroom. Darker colors help to hide marks left by wheelchairs, but unpatterned dark floors show dust and footprints. Dark colors also absorb light, a consideration for clients with vision differences who require increased lighting.

Hard surfaces must be slip resistant or treated with a nonskid wax. Test slipping with a crutch angled at approximately 70° from the horizontal. If the floor is rated as a nonskid surface, it should have a friction coefficient no less than .6 (.8 for ramps) when wet or dry.[9] A rubber floor often exceeds this criterion and is a good selection, especially in a design with a slightly raised disk or strip. A rubber floor will also lightly cushion falls.

5-18

TILE FLOORS

Textured quarry tile, especially in small sizes with many joints, is a good choice for the kitchen and offers better traction than shiny ceramic tiles. Rougher ceramic mosaic tile also provides good friction for wheeling but requires more strength to traverse than a synthetic floor without joints. Deep joints in a width greater than 3/4 in may hold the wheel of a wheelchair. Protruding joints may produce a washboardlike effect, which can cause extreme discomfort, pain, or spasticity for the wheelchair user. Cobblestones and uneven surfaces may resist rolling. Tile floors also increase the chance of breakage from kitchen accidents, but tile can be a good choice for traction and durability. (Fig. 5-18)

Irregular paving and flooring materials look as if they provide good traction, but they may cause tripping, especially for users of mobility aids. Ceramic mosaic tile can offer good traction without irregularities. Select a tile with an abrasive face, such as silicon carbide, carborundum, or grit. (Fig. 5-19) A slightly raised pattern will also reduce slipping. Keep the joints small between the tiles to prevent tripping. (Fig. 5-20)

5-19

5-20

 Use a moisture-resistant grout and vitreous tile where moisture is present and bacteria could grow. Porcelain, ceramic mosaic, and paver tiles are the most resistant to moisture.[10] Set the tile in portland cement; this is especially important in high-traffic areas or wet conditions where mastic is never recommended. A mixture of latex and portland cement is less permeable and should be used for shower stalls and other areas that may remain wet. The same mixture should be used in the grout. A grout in a darker color will not discolor as easily. (Fig. 5-21)

5-21

6. Furniture

Ⓤ Many beautiful barrier-free furnishings have never been used to meet the needs of people with different abilities. Instead, they have been hidden in catalogs or specified for their artistic value without an understanding of the contribution they could make to accessibility. Actually, this has been a blessing in disguise, since these products have never been stigmatized with "handicapped or elderly labels." They are products that meet the needs of all people while providing critical support to a few.

Ⓤ Manufacturers are only beginning to realize the potential of the market controlled by people with different abilities. This market is looking for products that can be easily managed and that can make everyday tasks easier to do and more enjoyable, not products that are complicated or bothersome to use.

B E D S

Ⓤ A comfortable bed and adequate storage are basic design elements of any bedroom, but these criteria become critical for clients with different abilities. Some simply spend more time in bed. Others find it difficult to sleep without pain or even to turn over in bed. A comfortable sleeping system with storage within reach becomes a necessity. (Fig. 6-1)

Specify a twin bed—its edges are easier to grip for turning. A shorter bed will provide additional space for wheelchair access. Many older people are comfortable with a 66-in youth bed. A fitted bedspread will not catch in the wheelchair mechanism. (Fig. 6-2)

6-1

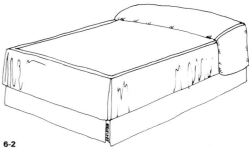

6-2

The height and stability of bedroom furniture are important considerations for wheelchair use. If the bed is too low for wheelchair transfer, consider adding locking casters or recess the legs in wooden blocks to raise the bed to the height of the wheelchair. Recess drawers' base under the bed, thus providing toe space for wheelchair use. (Fig. 6-3)

6-3

For clients who cannot transfer from bed, a system is available combining a hospital bed, a conveyor sheet, and a special wheelchair. The sheet carries the client to the foot of the bed and slides the user into a special wheelchair. It can also pick up the client out of the chair and slide the user back into bed. (Fig. 6-4)

Consider the installation of ceiling eyebolts above the bed for trapezes, tracks, frames, or lifts to aid in transfer or a change of position in bed. This installation is difficult to remove, however, and requires structural support. As an alternative, attach a trapeze to the headboard. Many people avoid the installation of a trapeze, however, because it visually calls attention to the differences of the user.

If side rails are used on the bed, they should be removable for ease of entry and exit. Latches for the side rails should be within reach, not at the foot of the bed. They should be below mattress level to prevent injury in transfer.

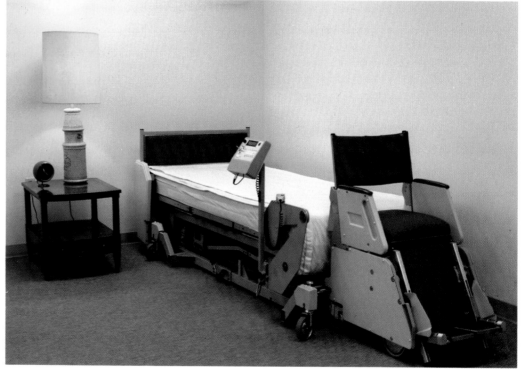

6-4

6-5

6-6

Consider a hospital bed to provide a raised angle for sleeping. Clients who are not susceptible to pressure sores can elevate their knees to relieve lumbar pressure. Elevated beds can also be helpful to clients with respiratory ailments or nausea. A hospital bed, however, may symbolize sickness and dependence on institutional care. For home use, some designs are more residential in appearance than others. (Fig. 6-5)

For clients with motion differences, specify footboards (in a height of 33 to 38 in) to provide stability when walking around the bed. The footboard can also be used to hold the blanket or bedspread to relieve pressure on the feet. (Fig. 6-6) Consider non-skids to stabilize footboards and other furniture; also make sure the various pieces are of substantial weight for stability. A headboard with an upper edge approximately 10 in above the mattress level may be used for support to rise to a standing position.

6-7

A stable headboard with vertical spindles can also be used for support when transferring. (Fig. 6-7) A headboard with built-in compartments or shelves can hold television controls, clocks, telephones, communication devices, bed controls, and alarm systems.

MATTRESSES

A mattress should provide good heat retention, offer sufficient absorption to allow ventilation, and be flame-retardant. It should be firm, featuring pocket coil springs or open coil springs with little side play. Plywood under the mattress serves as a good back support. The mattress cover should be changeable and washable. People with allergies often require cotton box spring covers and mattresses with cotton batting and ticking. People with limited circulation may prefer to sleep on sheepskin because the fleece serves as a soft support, conforming to the body and improving ventilation and absorption. The sheepskin should be washable.

Many water beds are manufactured from polyvinylchloride and other soft plastics that outgas, especially when heated. People with allergies may need to avoid these sleep systems, along with the algicides and fungicides often used with them.

Although a water bed offers good back support and evenly distributes weight to prevent bedsores, it also offers poor ventilation and presents difficulty in transferring. A better choice might be another system that evenly distributes weight. Systems are also available that allow a person to lie motionless while the mattress adapts to simulate position changes. All mattress systems should be evaluated for ease of transfer to and from a wheelchair and for dressing in bed. Specify a mattress with a firm edge at a 16-in height to help in transferring.[1] When using an adjustable bed, choose a mattress that does not "bunch" and become lumpy at the bends.

For a client who depends on the sense of touch more than vision, keep the mattress and nightstand at equal heights. Also, keep the dresser and headboard at equal heights; this way the client can slide a hand across the headboard to the dresser to locate objects.

NIGHTSTANDS

Specify a nightstand large enough to store a prosthesis. A gallery rail or edge around the top will prevent items from being accidently pushed to the floor. (Fig. 6-8)

Brightly colored furniture will offer a high contrast for a client who has vision differences. Clutter makes it difficult to spot things easily, so plan extra storage to prevent clutter.

For wheelchair access, specify a console or wall-mounted countertop to use as a nightstand with clearance for wheelchair footrests, making it easier to approach the bed or answer the phone. If a drawer is used, consider specifying a lock for privacy.

DRESSERS

In selecting a dresser, drawers are a good indication of quality. As a test for ease of use, grasp one corner and see if the drawer can be opened easily. Look for hardware that can be operated with a closed fist or slightly opened hand. To allow one-handed use, look for drawers narrow enough to open with one central C grip (Fig. 6-9) Drawers under the bed may be handy for clients who dress while seated or lying on the bed.

6-8

6-9

WARDROBES

A wardrobe on wheels can be used to move clothing and shoes to a dressing area. This is particularly helpful for clients who dress on the bed. Hooks and hangers in wardrobes should be adjustable down to at least 4 ft, although a 3-ft height is preferable. The 3-ft height is also good for children. (Fig. 6-10) A locking drawer in the wardrobe is a handy feature.

BED TABLES

A cantilever table that projects over the bed lets clients with reach differences work in bed. (Fig. 6-11) Specify a model that can fit under an adjustable bed with box springs or that can attach to the headboard.

Another choice could be a table that fits over the bed. Some models are adjustable for reading, writing, and working. (Fig. 6-12) A lazy susan on a large bed table can offer easier reach.

6-11

6-10

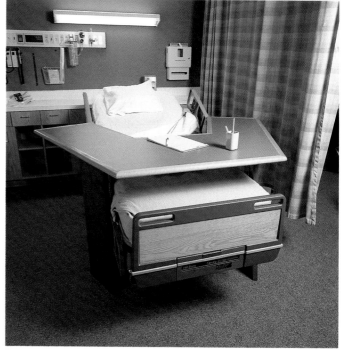
6-12

6-13

BOOKCASES

In choosing bookcases, consider flexibility and ease of maintenance. Custom features available include carpet casters, adjustable shelves, and interior lights (a feature that is particularly helpful to people with vision differences). (Fig. 6-13)

Because laminate finishes can chip, consider using distressed finishes, which hide abrasions. Oiled wood finishes can be touched up if abraded by wheelchairs. Metal trim can guard against chipping.

Look for rounded corners on case goods. The General Services Administration (GSA) Federal Supply Service required all furniture corners and edges to be rounded to a minimum $1/8$ in. Rounded corners are especially good for clients with vision problems and those who bruise easily. (Fig. 6-14)

6-14

U People often use bookcases for support when walking or transferring to a wheelchair, so structural integrity is important. Cabinet quality should be tested with a full load of storage. When the cabinet is pushed to the side, it should not sway or creak as if the joints are spreading. The back of the piece should be glued, screwed, and finished, but glue smeared around a joint indicates poor craftsmanship. Interiors of cabinets, shelves, and drawers should be light colored to increase visibility. Angled storage shelves should have raised edges to prevent items from slipping.

U Adjustable shelves in cabinets, bookcases, and other storage units offer maximum accessibility and flexibility as needs change. Consider a pulley system that allows shelves to be adjusted to various levels. Shallow shelves are more convenient for reach, especially from a wheelchair; they should be no deeper than 12 in when placed above shoulder level. A shelf with a 12-in depth can be further divided into two bypassing shelves. High shelves should be of glass, wire mesh, or clear plastic so that objects can be seen from below. This becomes critical with wheelchair use. (Fig. 6-15)

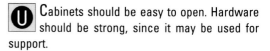 For wheelchair access, shelves should be at a reachable height, not to exceed 54 in from a side approach. Specify sliding cabinet doors or bifold doors that can swing out of the way of the wheelchair.

U Cabinets should be easy to open. Hardware should be strong, since it may be used for support.

ROOM DIVIDERS

U With proper furniture planning, large spaces will not appear institutional. Room dividers, hanging wall systems, and screens may help to temporarily divide a space and still free it for a variety of later uses. Dividers can also help to define territory or set up a transition between spaces. (Fig. 6-16) Avoid partitions with legs that extend into traffic areas. The legs can pose a tripping hazard and can limit wheelchair access.

6-15

6-16

Ventilation to control heat buildup and odor is an important feature if the room divider will be used to store a television, computer, or appliance. If the client has allergies, the odors from the equipment may have to be vented outdoors.

To maximize strength, raise work surfaces so that bending is not required. Heavier items like televisions can be more easily managed on swing-out shelves or turntables. Books are easier to grasp on shallow shelves, with the books protruding slightly. Deep shelves and clothing racks should roll out. (Fig. 6-17)

WALL SYSTEMS

Wall systems with adjustable shelves, drawers, and cabinets allow storage heights to be customized to the reach of the client, which is especially important for wheelchair access. Store seldom-used objects at the extreme edges of the range of reach. (Fig. 6-18)

Freestanding wall systems that are open on both sides are more convenient than cabinets opening on one side only. Such systems can lessen the need for movement.

Pull-out shelves and drop-lid desks are available on many wall systems, offering the option of lower work surfaces for use from a wheelchair. Surfaces at elbow height are useful for fine, discrete manipulations, such as writing.

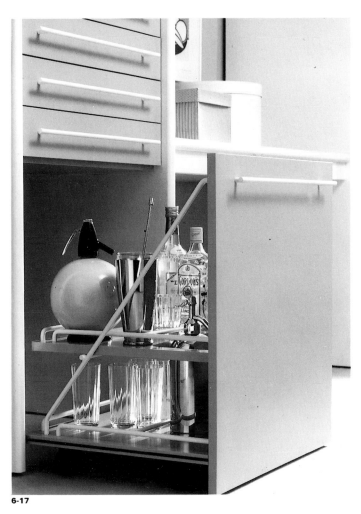

6-17

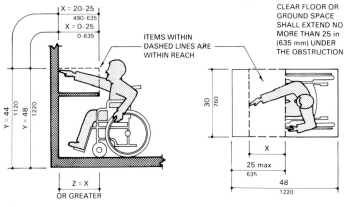

NOTE: x = Reach distance, y = Maximum height, z = Clear knee space. z is the clear space below the obstruction, which shall be at least as deep as the reach distance, x.

6-18   *Maximum Forward Reach over an Obstruction*

6-19

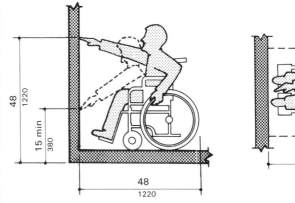

6-20

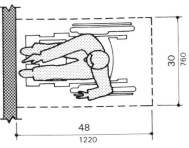

Forward Reach Limit

People with coordination differences find it easier to work on surfaces slightly below elbow height. For people in wheelchairs, cabinets and drawers must be raised at least 9 in from the floor to allow footrest clearance. (Fig. 6-19)

Keep drawers in wall systems at a reachable height (under 32 in). Clients in wheelchairs may have trouble reaching to the back of drawers that are installed any higher.

A wall-mounted shelf for phone books is handy beneath a wall phone, which should be installed within reach. Add a clip to the shelf to secure a notepad. For planning shelf heights and depths, consider the maximum reach of the client in a wheelchair. (Fig. 6-20)

Wall-mounted shelves for parcels are helpful near a door. Install them on the latch side of the door at elbow height or slightly above the wheelchair armrest. A shelf may be needed on both the inside and outside of the doorway.

With a wall bed system, an extra bed can be added without limiting space for wheelchair access. Some models offer a power system to raise and lower the bed. (Fig. 6-21) Be sure to specify an extendable nightstand, or cut portholes in the side of the system to allow the nightstand to be reached from bed.

6-21

TABLES

 Basic features to consider in table selection include construction, surface reflection, and height to support the task. These become critical for clients who may need to lean on the table for support, are susceptible to surface glare, or require specific heights to meet their needs.

A sturdy table may be necessary for support. When evaluating table construction, look for blocking in the leg joints. The joints should also be glued and screwed. Consistency of the type of wood used is a sign of quality construction.

Table and desk surfaces should reflect from 30 to 50 percent of light. Darker woods, including rosewood and walnut, reflect as little as 9 percent. A white top reflects too much light and can tire the eyes. Shiny and glossy surfaces also produce too much glare. Select dull greens and beiges or light oak, maple, cherry, and teak for proper light reflectance.[2] (Fig. 6-22)

6-23

A round or oval top on a pedestal base allows an approach from all directions. (Fig. 6-23) Specify a stable base which will support a person who leans on the edge of the top.

Select a table with a border clearly identifying the edge. A raised edge will keep spills off the floor. (Fig. 6-24) Specify a round table or a table without sharp corners to prevent bruising. An adjustable-height table will allow a client to raise the table for detailed projects and reading.

Natural oak
Natural oak veneer

Planked maple

Colonial cherry

6-22

6-24

In the dining room, a 60-in round table can comfortably seat six, including one person in a wheelchair. If the diameter is increased to 66 in, seven can be seated, including one person in a wheelchair. Eight can be seated around a 72-in table, including one person in a wheelchair. These estimates are based on dining room chairs that are 23 in wide.

A square table (54 by 54 in) can seat four people in wheelchairs. For rectangular tables, allow 24 in for each dining chair and 30 in for each wheelchair. (Fig. 6-25) Children's tables should be adjustable. (Fig. 6-26)

The size, height, shape of the top, and type of base may all limit the approach from a wheelchair. Children require a knee space of 24 in[3] from the underside of the table to the floor. Low cross bars between table legs may prohibit wheelchair access. Cross bars should be recessed a minimum of 19 in from the front edge of the table. Skirt boards should be recessed a minimum of 12 in.[4] Trestle tables are often high enough to meet these requirements.

Pedestal tables allow closer access if the base does not interfere with the wheelchair footrests. Bases must be heavily weighted to prevent accidental overturning.

A table with legs is more stable than a table with a pedestal base. Rubber or upholstered legs resist wheelchair abrasion. (Fig. 6-27) A table with a minimum clearance of 27 in allows a wheelchair to slide under the table apron. Specify a high table (in the range of 32 to 36 in) for a closer wheelchair approach. A high table facilitates use of the shoulders and upper arms. If it is too high, however, it may put pressure on the back and cause eye strain.

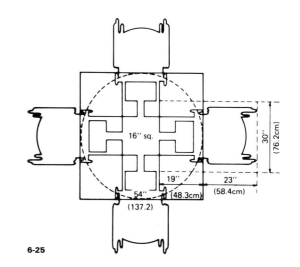

6-25

6-26

6-27

6-28

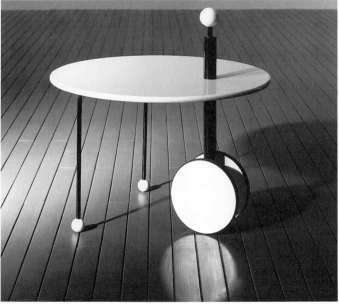

6-29

U For larger projects, plan an adjustable work-table. For a person in a wheelchair one large table is more accessible than a grouping of smaller tables. For smaller projects, consider an adjustable coffee table. (Fig. 6-28) This works well for clients who choose to spend some time on the floor out of the wheelchair. High coffee tables (21 to 24 in) do not pose a tripping hazard,[5] but low tables are easier to reach from a seated position.

U Avoid table legs or supports that extend into traffic areas. Keep coffee tables lightweight or on casters if they are to be pushed out of the way for wheelchair passage. (Fig. 6-29) A nest of lightweight tables can be stacked out of the way when not in use. (Fig. 6-30)

6-30

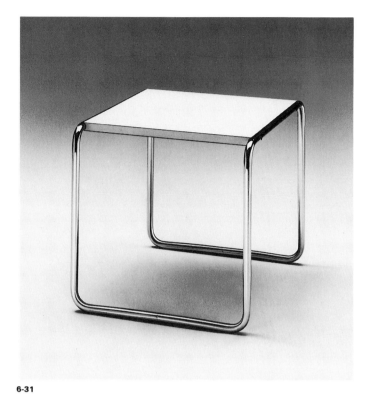

6-31

Pedestal coffee tables cannot be used for support when sitting down or rising from the sofa, and drop leaves will not support much weight. Choose a well-constructed table with straight legs for support. Sleigh legs are easier to move over textured surfaces. (Fig. 6-31)

Lamp tables and side tables are often moved; they should be lightweight and mobile. For detailed work from a standing position, keep the table slightly below elbow height. Heavy manual work requires a table about 10 in below elbow height.[6]

In planning reachability, consider the shape of the table. With a 60- by 30-in table, only 68 percent of the surface can be reached.[7] A person with mobility differences will use even less of the surface. An L- or U-shaped surface can bring all items within reach for many people, (Fig. 6-32) although the corners may still be difficult.

6-32

A drop-leaf table leaves the space clear for wheelchair turns when closed. (Fig. 6-33) To save space, use a drop-leaf table as a sofa table that can be extended for dining. Be sure the space between the legs is wide enough (30 in) for a wheelchair approach. (Fig. 6-34) Extra seating stored under a sofa table can save space for wheelchair passage. (Fig. 6-35)

6-33

6-34

6-35

6-36

6-37

U Flip-top tables can be stacked against the wall to clear the space for wheelchair passage. (Fig. 6-36, 6-37) Specify locking casters so that tables can be moved for storage. A wall-mounted table that folds flat against the wall can also help keep space clear for wheelchair passage.

U For serving food or clearing a table, specify a small cart. A toaster or microwave can also be moved on the cart from the kitchen to the dining room. (Fig. 6-38) Another handy item is a carpeted exercise table or bench at the height of the wheelchair to allow easy transfer. This elevated bench also works well for people with mobility differences who have trouble getting up from the floor after exercising. (Fig. 6-39)

6-38

6-39

6-40

DESKS

U For typing, the desk surface should be between $5\frac{1}{2}$ and 7 in above seat height. (Fig. 6-40) For most other tasks, the surface should be between 10 and 12 in from seat height.[8] Desks with adjustable slanting tops can reduce fatigue and discomfort.[9] (Fig. 6-41, 6-42)

6-41

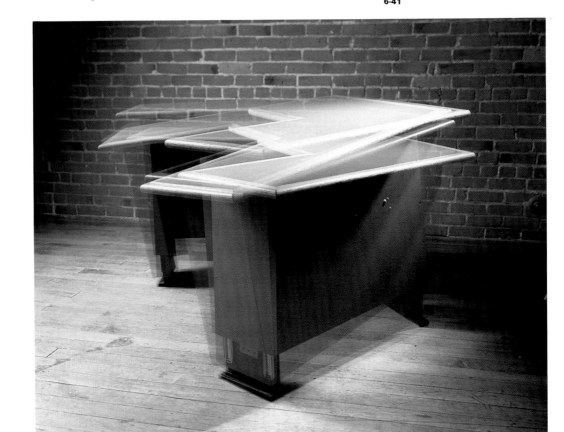

6-42

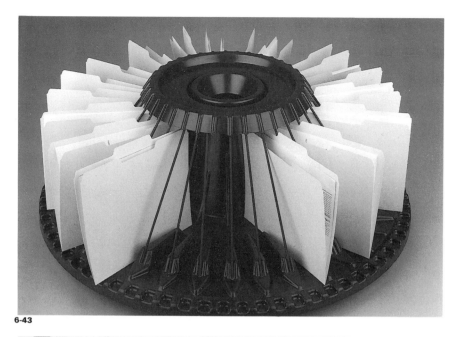

6-43

Specify a desk with removable cutouts for a closer wheelchair approach. Some models offer high rims to keep items from rolling off, and others offer a built-in lazy susan. (Fig. 6-43)

Consider using a hunt table as a desk, which offers access to a larger surface area. The surface on all sides also provides extra support for arms and shoulders.

Pedestal desks allow easier wheelchair approaches than do desks with legs. Movable file cabinets under the desk can prevent extra trips across the room. The top of a cabinet can be used as extra workspace when the file is rolled out. For clients who need to lean on a file cabinet for stability, (Fig. 6-44) specify a model with locking casters.

6-44

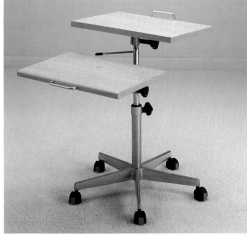

6-45

Ⓤ Plan an adjustable-height workstation for computer use. Make sure the keyboard shelf or table can be adjusted to just barely clear the lap. Position the center of the screen slightly below eye level for maximum visual acuity. Looking up at a screen can cause neck discomfort over an extended period of time. (Fig. 6-45)

Ⓤ When specifying a reception desk in an office, keep a section at wheelchair height (30 to 34 in), with clearance of 27 in below. An accessible width of 42 in should be allowed.[10] This allows direct visual access between the staff and other visitors. (Fig. 6-46)

6-46

FRAME SEATING

U In planning seating, consider comfort, quality of construction, and ease of maintenance. A comfortable chair should allow the client to place both feet flat on the floor. (Fig. 6-47) Most of the weight should be on the buttocks, and there should be a space between the thigh and front edge of the seat. Pressure behind the thigh over an extended period of time could aggravate circulation problems.[11]

U The deeper the seat, the more slant needed on the backrest for comfort. An open space between the seat and the back is often more comfortable, since it allows extra room for the buttocks. (Fig. 6-48) The back of the chair should be adjustable from 8 to 13 in from the seat surface. Plan chairs in a variety of sizes to accommodate both small and large visitors. (The width of the seat should be no less than 16 in and the depth no less than 15 in.)[12] A variety of styles can be used as markers to help people become oriented in large commercial spaces.

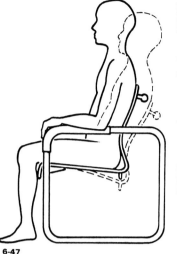

6-47

U In a chair without armrests, the client will be more comfortable if the back of the chair is narrower than the width of the shoulders and lower than the shoulder blades. In a chair with armrests, the client should be able to rest naturally on the arms, although lower armrests may be better with a desk or table. The armrests should be slightly below the table apron.

U Specify at least one chair in which the client can be comfortable for a long period of time. For comfort, the seat may have to be adjusted in height (between $13^2/_3$ and $20^2/_3$ in).[13] (Fig. 6-49) The angle of the seat and backrest should also be adjustable. Pressure on the spine decreases as the tilt of the backrest increases. A lumbar cushion also reduces pressure and offers greater support.

6-48

6-49

6-50

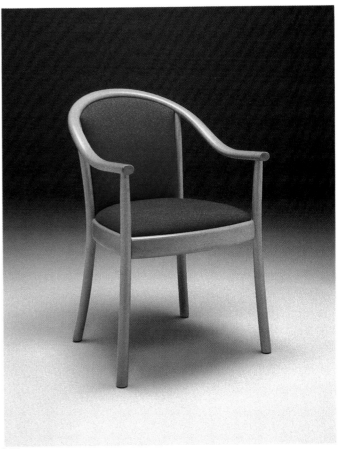

A high stool may help the client maintain endurance and strength with minimal bending over a task. (Fig. 6-50) The client may also want higher dining chairs (with a seat height of 18 in). A lower height may be hard on knees and hips when getting up and down from the chair. The seat cushion should compress no more than 1 in.[14]

Armrests should seldom be higher than 8½ in above the seat for maximum support and reduction of fatigue. Armrests alone support 12.4 percent of body weight.[15] They offer a sense of greater security and provide support in rising from the chair. Many people get out of a chair by first sliding forward to the edge and then pushing off. A chair with an armrest that swivels up facilitates wheelchair transfers. (Fig. 6-51) Make sure that the chair will not tip forward and that the arms extend slightly beyond the leading edge of the chair seat. Low bracing interferes with rising from a chair if a client tucks his feet under the seat to push off. (Fig. 6-52)

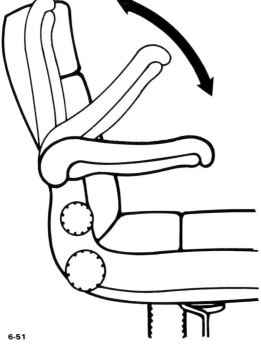

6-51

6-52

To provide extra support, specify seat stretchers. Stretchers also stabilize a chair for wheelchair transfer.

Hard, not padded, chair arms are helpful for transferring from a wheelchair. Look for chairs with firm seat cushioning. A cushion is especially helpful in the area where the spine meets the seat.

Proper cushioning will prevent skin ulcers. Test for proper cushioning by putting the full weight of your closed fist in the center of the seat. You should not feel a spring or supporting board. Upholstery that is too soft is not appropriate for work and can even induce sleep.[16]

Choose seating with curved edges, padded corners, and soft surfaces to prevent bruises and pressure on the backs of the knees. (Fig. 6-53) Removable cushion covers without welting, ridges, or tufts are easier to maintain. Welting at the front of the seat may hamper circulation to the legs.

Upholstery fabrics that allow the skin to breathe and prevent slipping will also make chairs more comfortable. Use nylon upholstery for abrasion resistance, polypropylene for stain and sun resistance (but not resistance to heat or stretching), and wool for porosity and comfort. Remember that vinyl or plastic coverings on chairs may become hot, slippery, and uncomfortable when used on upholstery planned for long-term seating. Shiny vinyl is associated with institutional use and will make an interior appear more sterile. Use a vinyl with a slight texture or pattern. (Fig. 6-54)

If the client is more comfortable with the hip or knee in a straight position, choose a chair with a movable thigh rest. Armrests are also available for supporting paralyzed arms.

6-53

EVALUATION GUIDE: PROPERTIES OF FIBERS

Property	Wool	Nylon	Modac	Olefin	Cotton	Rayon	Acryl	Poly
Strength	2	4	3	*	4	*	3	*
Flexibility	5	3	3	4	3	3	3	4
Resiliency	4	5	5	4	2	2	5	3
Extensibility	4	4	4	*	2	2	4	4
Recovery	3	5	3	3	1	1	3	5
Elasticity	4	4	3	3	2	2	3	4
Absorbency	4	2	2	2	4	4	2	1
Resistance to:								
Alkali	2	4	4	4	4	3	3	3
Acid	3	2	4	4	2	3	3	4
Solvents	4	4	4	2	4	4	4	4
Sun	1	1	5	3	3	1	5	3
Micro/Insects	1	5	5	5	1	1	5	5
Reaction to:								
Flame	BS	BS/M	M	B/M	BQ	BQ	BQ/M	BS/M
Flame removal	SE	SE	SE	CB	CB	CB	CB	SE

Abrasion resistance is a function of strength, flexibility and resiliency.

Dimensional stability is a function of resiliency, extensibility, recovery, elasticity and absorbency.

Legend:
* = dependent on formulation
5 = excellent or very high
4 = very good or high
3 = good or medium
2 = fair or low
1 = poor or very low

Modac = modacrylic
Acryl = acrylic
Poly = polyester

B = burns, S = slowly, Q = quickly, M = melts,
SE = self extinguishing, CB = continues burning

6-54

6-55

6-56

6-57

U A high-back rocker provides head support, but make sure the chair will not tip. (Fig. 6-55) Studies have shown that patients with dementia profit from access to chairs that rock or swivel.[17]

U Mobile stools allow a wide range of motion in places too tight for a wheelchair. Choose a stool with adjustable seat height, seat angle, armrest, backrest, and footrest. Casters that automatically lock during wheelchair transfer are also helpful. In addition, the hardware for chair adjustment should be easy to operate. (Fig. 6-56)

C Clients can maintain eye contact and read lips or gestures more easily from swivel chairs in a group situation. (Fig. 6-57) Semicircular seating arrangements are recommended, perhaps around a table.

U For people who are sensitive to petrochemicals, specify hardwood or metal furniture rather than composite wood or pressboard frames. Choose pieces with mechanical fasteners instead of glue.[18]

UPHOLSTERED SEATING

 Specify couches and chairs with firm cushions; a soft cushion will make wheelchair transfer difficult. Down cushions, for example, are too soft. If the deck is also too soft, add plywood under the cushion for support.

Bucket seats and some contour seats make it difficult to shift or change position. Rockers aid muscle tone, digestion, and circulation, but they should be locking to aid in transferring.

To easily rearrange the room, put casters on all furniture except those pieces used for transfer. Casters allow furniture to be pushed out of the way for wheelchair clearance.

To maximize strength, furniture and equipment should be selected on the basis of operation. Maximum effort can then be deployed when the greatest number of muscles are involved, when the largest muscles are used, and when muscles are resting at their length. For example, bend the knees to extend the large leg muscles to their length before lifting rather than using the weaker back muscles. Avoid furniture which involves unusual angles of exertion like sleeper sofas and reclining rockers.

If the client does not have the arm strength to operate the controls of a recliner but finds the automatic legrest convenient, consider a recliner with foot controls. (Fig. 6-58)

A recliner on casters allows the client to be pushed from one room to another on hard floors. (Fig. 6-59)

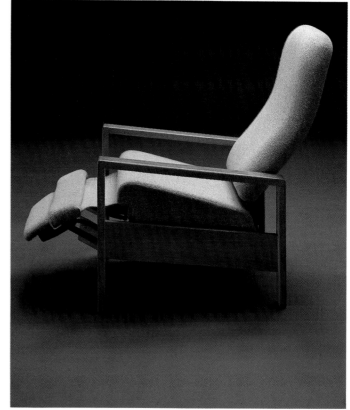

6-58

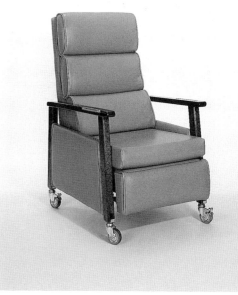

6-59

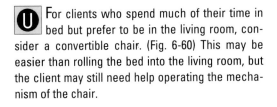 For clients who spend much of their time in bed but prefer to be in the living room, consider a convertible chair. (Fig. 6-60) This may be easier than rolling the bed into the living room, but the client may still need help operating the mechanism of the chair.

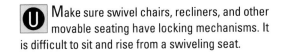 Make sure swivel chairs, recliners, and other movable seating have locking mechanisms. It is difficult to sit and rise from a swiveling seat.

Specify seats at the same height as a wheelchair to aid in transfer and to reduce the difference in eye level. If a chair or couch is too low for easy transfer, raise it with blocks of wood. Recess the sofa legs into the blocks for stability. Cover the blocks with a longer skirt or add a slipcover. If the seating extends to the floor, make sure the base is recessed for wheelchair footrests. (Fig. 6-61)

6-60

6-61

Many people lean on upholstered seating for support while standing. The legs of a sofa or chair should be at the corners of the seat. The back legs should extend outward so the feet are even with the top of the backrest. (Fig. 6-62)

Clients with strength differences may have trouble rising from the center cushion of a long sofa. A shorter sofa allows more flexibility in furniture arrangement and puts the client closer to an armrest for support when rising. (Fig. 6-63) Add a portable lift seat to an existing chair to help the client rise slowly to a 45° angle. Or consider a chair with a controlled pneumatic lift. Models are available with movable seats and armrests.

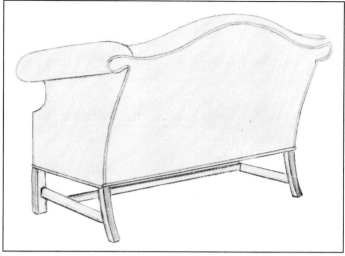

6-62

6-63

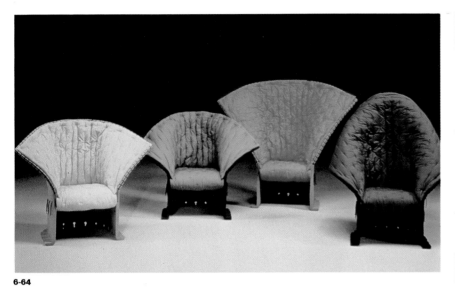

6-64

6-65

Ⓤ A high-back chair can provide protection from drafts and a feeling of greater security, (Fig. 6-64) but lightweight, open chairs usually occupy less floor space and are easily moved. If the client naps in the chair, look for an adjustable head cushion. Unless the chair is very low to the floor, the client may need a footrest. (Fig. 6-65) For clients with back problems, choose a footrest that is high enough to keep the knees bent at a height slightly above the waist. When choosing a footrest, make sure it is easily removable. Low ottomans can pose a tripping hazard. Keep these well away from high-traffic areas.

Ⓤ Many clients with different abilities will be slow in responding to a fire, so fire-resistant furnishings become critical. Most states require testing for flammability. California Technical Bulletin 133 requires that the product as a whole be tested rather than its individual components. Rate of temperature increase, the amount of toxic gas produced, smoke density, and weight loss of the test sample burned may be affected by combinations of fabric, cushion, and construction. Designs with open arms and backs, for example, may be rated differently than designs with loose seat and back cushions with upholstered arms.[19]

Ⓤ Do not try to improve the rating by applying chemical flame retardants to the fabric. They have not been proven effective and may even produce toxic gases when burned. These may also change the appearance of the fabric.

For clients with coordination differences, select upholstered pieces with soft corners. Avoid slippery fabrics; choose textured fabrics with corrugation for more friction. The latter can help disoriented clients maintain an upright sitting position for extended periods of time.[20] Slippery fabrics are used to help weaker clients slide into deep booths or auto interiors.

7. Accessories and Equipment

The value of a building design may be determined by the attention to detail. Is there a paper cup dispenser next to the water fountain? Can room accessories be personalized? Is the telephone equipped with amplification? Does the alarm clock have large lighted numerals? Can controls be operated with a closed fist? Does the interior reflect care and concern?

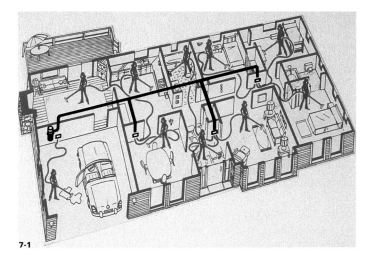

7-1

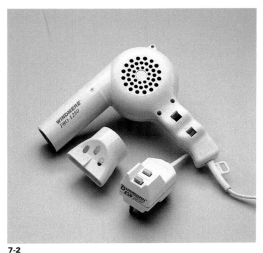

7-2

SMALL APPLIANCES

U Cordless units can save time and energy. They can be operated from a distance by touch control, by phone, or with voice signals. For people with differences in ability, appliance controls must be carefully selected and installed to make sure units are usable. For clients in wheelchairs, controls for appliances should be set at counter level. With smart appliances, like built-in vacuum systems, controls are eliminated. A vacuum system of this type is especially convenient for clients in wheelchairs; the hose is simply inserted into the inlet to start operation. Be sure to mount the inlet at a reachable height (15 in). (Fig. 7-1) A built-in vacuum system is also appropriate for people with allergies, since dust and other allergens are blown out of the house.

If the cost of a built–in vacuum is not in the budget, a portable vacuum can be strapped to the back of a wheelchair for easier use.

U A cordless rechargeable vacuum cleaner saves time and the effort involved in hauling out a large vacuum and maneuvering around the cord. It also improves reach from a wheelchair when a quick cleanup is in order. Consider an upright vacuum for people with coordination differences who may have difficulty pushing down on a hand-held hose.

Appliance safety features become critical for people with coordination differences. For example, a hand-held hair dryer could be dropped into the bathtub or sink. Select small appliances that offer such features as a ground fault circuit interrupter to prevent electrical shock. (Fig. 7-2)

Some small appliances are specifically geared for differences in ability. They can make life easier and also more enjoyable. An electric easel, for example, allows people who use a mouth stick to draw or paint. With the touch of a button or joystick, the canvas moves up, down, or to either side.

For people who are blind, books are available on tape. A tape player with earphones and a remote control or foot petal can also be helpful. This can be used by blind people in place of notes when public speaking.

For people with vision differences, alarm clocks are available with extra-large numerals that can be brightened or dimmed as needed. (Fig. 7-3) Talking alarm clocks announce the time in a humanlike voice. (Fig. 7-4) Talking wristwatches are available with an alarm. (Fig. 7-5) Talking scales announce current weight as well as any weight gain or loss. For convenience look for models with toe-operated controls. (Fig. 7-6)

For people with hearing differences, appliances are available that improve sound level without disturbing others. A cordless headset for televisions, for instance, increases the volume without increasing the noise level in the room.

7-3

7-4

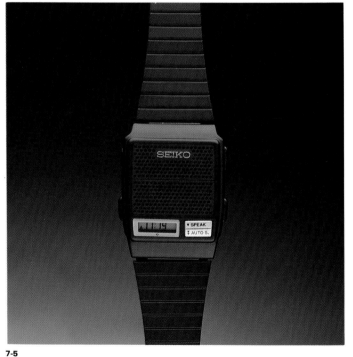

7-5

7-6

OFFICE EQUIPMENT

🅤 Office equipment must be specified to improve accessibility for employees. Copying machines, for example, should be no higher than 30 in. Touch controls should be located toward the front of the machine, and a clear floor space should be provided to access the controls, load paper into the machine, make copies, and retrieve documents.

🅤 Slide projectors and other office equipment with wireless remote controls are convenient for all people, especially those with differences in ability. Be aware that most stands for slide projectors are too high for people in wheelchairs; a height adjustment may be needed. The projector can be stored in pop-up stands for easy access. (Fig. 7-7)

Calculators, automatic pencil sharpeners, and many other pieces of office equipment have been designed for one-handed use. Typewriters can now be added to that list. In selecting a model, specify right- or left-handed use. (Fig. 7-8)

COMPUTERS

🅤 Computers are used for a wide range of daily activities: telephoning, messaging, banking, and shopping, to name a few. Computer use does not require verbal communication, a decided advantage for people with hearing or speech differences. Computers offer "bulletin boards," networks, and direct communication with anyone who has a touch-tone phone or a text telephone for the deaf.[1] (Fig. 7-9)

7-7

7-8

7-9

A variety of accessories are available for computer use with a mouth stick or with one hand. Keylatches are helpful for people who have trouble pressing two computer keys at the same time. A keyguard or wristguard stabilizes the finger, hand, or stick so that other keys are not pressed by accident. (Fig. 7-10) Some computer programs don't require users to press two keys simultaneously, as with shift and control keys. Others allow the keyboard position to be redefined. Still others slow down or eliminate the "auto-repeat" feature, which may be difficult to control.[2]

Keyboards are available with larger keys for people with coordination differences. Some have single keys for frequently used words and phrases. For people who cannot depress keys, membrane keyboards are available. Switching systems can be operated by any movement and are used to replace keyboards. Switches are used in conjunction with a scanner or with Morse code, which is faster than scanning. Scanners provide wide choices of information on a screen or separate panel. The user selects the information of interest with a switch. Voice-recognition systems are also available that accept spoken commands.[3]

People with learning impairments profit from the immediate feedback offered by computers. (Fig. 7-11) Learners see, hear, and feel information (on a touch screen) to reinforce the message and allow for different learning styles.

A speech synthesizer offers voice output for a client who cannot use the screen or who has a speech impairment. The computerized voice lets the user hear the information printed on the screen. It provides immediate audio feedback as data is entered, so mistakes are easily identified.[4]

Screen magnifiers, braille systems, and optical readers are helpful add-ons for many people with differences in vision. Printed information can be scanned and displayed on a magnified screen, reprinted in braille, or "read" by the speech synthesizer. This is especially helpful for dated information like newspapers or correspondence that needs attention before a tape or reading service can be used.[5]

Computers are becoming more user friendly for people with different abilities. A printer system, for example, can be operated with a mouth stick or a hand with limited function. Typing wheels and ribbon cartridges can be changed easily and the platen turned without difficulty. One excellent example of a user-friendly device is a disk-loading system that lets a computer be operated fully with a mouth stick.

7-10

7-11

DRINKING FOUNTAINS AND WATER COOLERS

U Blind people who use canes cannot detect water coolers with floor clearances exceeding 27 in.[6] People in wheelchairs require a clearance of at least 27 in, so this must be the exact clearance to meet the needs of both populations. Built-in units can have higher clearances without becoming obstacles for people with vision differences. A recessed fountain or cooler should optimally be between 17 and 19 in deep. The recess should be a minimum of 30 in wide and a maximum of 24 in deep. (Fig. 7-12)

U A second recessed water fountain or cooler for children should be installed with a spout no higher than 30 in and a clear knee space of 24 in.[7] The spout of a water fountain for adults should be no higher than 36 in. (Fig. 7-13) It should be located close to the front of the unit with a water flow parallel to the front edge. The flow should be at least 4 in high for use with a cup. A paper cup dispenser adjacent to the water fountain allows use by many people who have differences in reach and coordination.

U Controls should be located near the front edge of the fountain. They should be operable with one hand without pinching, tight grasping, or twisting of the wrist. (Fig. 7-14) An automatic sensor is most easily operated.

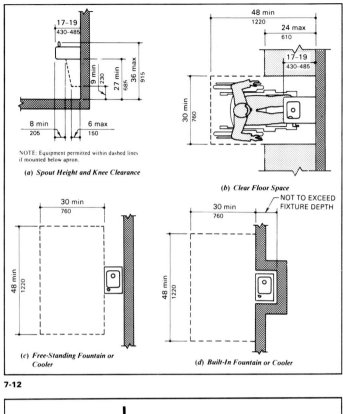

(a) *Spout Height and Knee Clearance*

NOTE: Equipment permitted within dashed lines if mounted below apron.

(b) *Clear Floor Space*

(c) *Free-Standing Fountain or Cooler*

(d) *Built-In Fountain or Cooler*

7-12

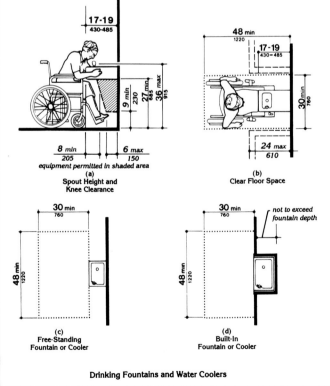

(a)
Spout Height and
Knee Clearance

equipment permitted in shaded area

(b)
Clear Floor Space

(c)
Free-Standing
Fountain or Cooler

(d)
Built-In
Fountain or Cooler

Drinking Fountains and Water Coolers

7-13

7-14

TELEPHONES

U The simple telephone has now become a machine that understands specific voices, takes notes, communicates with others, and travels everywhere. When used as a component of a "smart" house, the phone can open doors, adjust heating and cooling, start the oven, and dim the lights. If water in a kettle is boiling on the stove, the level of the flame on the range can be lowered by a phone call from bed. One phone call can warm up the hot tub and start a romantic fire using a gas log in the fireplace.

U If a forward reach is required, an accessible telephone must be at a height no greater than 4 ft. Keep the route to the phone free of obstacles, and allow a 30- by 48-in clear space for a wheelchair approach in front of it. (Fig. 7-15) The bottom of the phone and or its wall guard must be no more than 27 in above the floor. (Fig. 7-16) Phones placed higher cannot be detected by blind people using canes. Recessed telephones and directories work well for people with vision differences, as well as for people in wheelchairs, providing the recess is a minimum of 30 in wide and a maximum of 24 in deep with a clear floor space.[8]

U If the existing wall phone is in an awkward location, replace it with a remote control portable phone. For people with motion differences, portable phones can prevent the race to the telephone or the frustration of a missed phone call. Choose a model with a two-way intercom for communication between the base unit and the handset. Specify a phone that searches frequencies for the clearest channel and switches between tone and pulse for use with a computer. Other features to consider are automatic redial, volume control, and a ringer that cannot be heard through the earpiece.

U A car phone is a convenience as well as a necessary security feature for people of all abilities. Many public phones are not accessible. With a car phone, help can be reached, appointments can be confirmed, and directions can be requested, resulting in a great savings of time and energy.

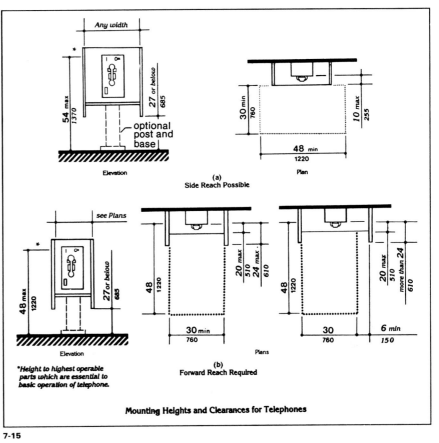

Height to highest operable parts which are essential to basic operation of telephone.

Mounting Heights and Clearances for Telephones

7-15

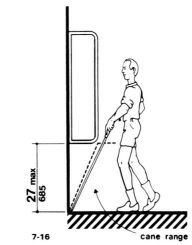

7-16

cane range

U Touch controls on phones are easier to manipulate for people with differences in coordination. Card-dial telephones are also available. Touch controls on the headset are more convenient for use from bed. (Fig. 7-17) Make sure the cord to the handset will reach across the width of the bed and wall-mount lighter-weight phones for additional stability. Specify a cord length of at least 29 in between the handset and the base of all phones.[9]

Some telephones can be used with a light-sensitive probe. Models with larger, easy-to-read push buttons are also available. (Fig. 7-18)

If touch controls are still too difficult, attach a touch plate. Pressure on any part of the plate dials an operator, who will, in turn, place the call. Puff-and-sip dialing systems are available on some telephones; the operator is contacted by blowing into a plastic tube. (Fig. 7-19) Voice-activated dialers are also available. The phone responds to the spoken name of the person to be called, recalls the number, and dials it. (Fig. 7-20)

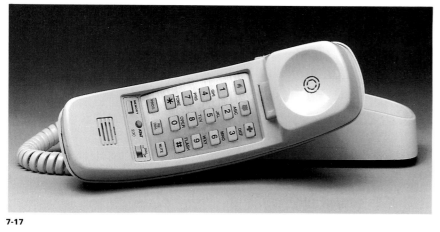

7-17

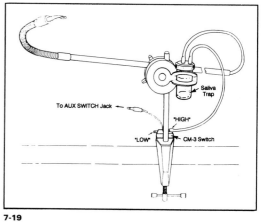

7-19

7-18

7-20

Headsets can be used by people with differences in arm motion or manual dexterity. Another alternative is a phone holder hand clip or shoulder phone. (Fig. 7-21) Also consider a telephone stand with a handset clamp. Some models have a lever-operated line interrupter that can be used by pushing with the hand, elbow, or foot. With the line interrupter, the handset can be left permanently in the clamp.

Light-touch speaker phones are useful for people with differences in strength. Speakers can also be attached to existing telephones. Models are available with touch tone, memory for automatic dialing, and an answering system. (Fig. 7-22)

For people with hearing differences, telephone receivers should generate a magnetic field to be compatible with many hearing aids. In-line amplifiers are available, and portable amplifiers can be added to an existing telephone. (Fig. 7-23) Amplified phones are also available with a volume control in the headset.

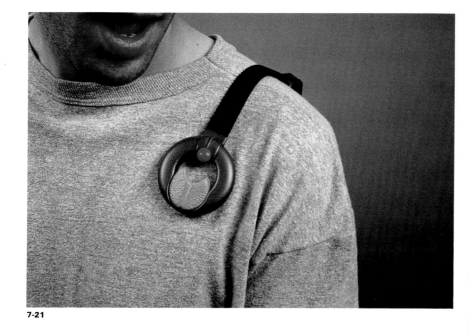

7-21

7-22

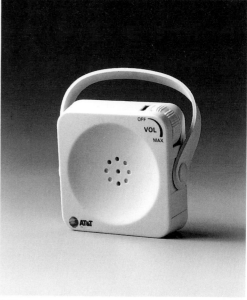

7-23

Text telephones, tone ringers, gongs, and signals in other frequencies allow more choices in signaling an incoming call. Telephones can also be wired to vibrators, room lights, flashing lights, or amplified signaling devices. (Fig. 7-24)

Telephones, teleprinters, and other telephonic devices are available to transmit printed messages to a teletype emphasis printer or television monitor. (Fig. 7-25) A portable text telephone can be used to call any location with a compatible unit or through a relay to a noncompatible unit. A built-in printer provides a record of the conversation, an advantage to all users. A less expensive text telephone provides a visual readout only.

For a client with a soft voice or with speech differences, consider a handset for speech amplification. It plugs into any modular telephone and increases the volume of the voice by as much as 30 percent. (Fig. 7-26)

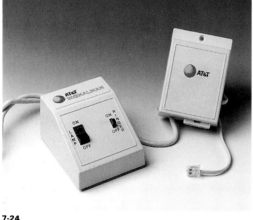

7-24

7-25

7-26

DECORATIVE ACCESSORIES

U Decorative accessories may actually reduce stress when the client maintains control of the selection and chooses a "positive distraction."[10] Art can be a source of relaxation and pleasure or a source of irritation, depending on the reaction of the client. The choice of art can be returned to the individual in a health care setting through a mobile cabinet or "art cart," which allows each person to personalize accessories in his or her room. A similar program can be introduced in an office setting or in any other space principally occupied by one user. (Fig. 7-27)

U Encourage clients to display wall hangings or crafts to personalize the interior. Use accessories that reflect the interests of the client. Collections can be displayed in curio cabinets or tables. (Fig. 7-28)

Hang some artwork and other wall-mounted accessories at eye level from a wheelchair. Include mirrors at wheelchair height in the bedroom and by the front door. Elevate glass at least 10 in from the floor to avoid damage from wheelchair footrests. (Fig. 7-29)

U For people with hearing impairments, avoid tall arrangements of flowers or accessories on furniture that block a clear line of vision to interpreters or other people in the room. Tall arrangements may make it more difficult to maintain eye contact, to read lips and gestures, to hear, or to be heard.

7-27

7-28

7-29

SIGNS

Signs in public spaces are needed to control movement and to offer advice, information, and identification. They are important elements of both wayfinding and orientation strategies. Signs must be understandable, requiring no further clarification.[11] Simple terms like "walkway" or "general hospital," for example, are more easily understood than "overhead link" or "medical pavilion."[12] Signs must be consistent throughout the space, as succinct as possible, readable for all users (composed at a sixth-grade reading level), and stated in positive terms.[13]

To identify accessible facilities and parking, use the international symbol for accessibility. (Fig. 7-30) Parking signs should directly face the driver within a 60° cone of vision.[14]

Contrast, proportion, and redundant cuing are important features. The top three color combinations for maximum contrast and visibility are black on yellow, (Fig. 7-31) black on white, and yellow on black, in that order.[15] People who are color-blind will have difficulty with signs relying on contrast between red and green.

Signs that offer tactile as well as visual cues are important to people with differences in vision. Tactile signs should include letters or symbols raised a minimum of $1/32$ in and should be accompanied with Grade 2 Braille.[16] Raised arabic numerals and standard block uppercase letters without serif are recommended.[17] Raised characters should be a minimum of $5/8$ in in height[18] but no higher than 2 in.[19]

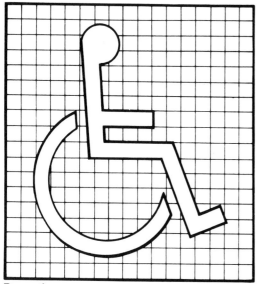

Proportions

7-30   **Display Conditions**

7-31

People with differences in vision require tactile signs that identify accessible routes, common use spaces (e.g., cafeterias), or public health and safety features (e.g., flashing alarms, fire exits, toilets, hazardous areas, and fire extinguishers). In the event of an emergency, exit signs should be backed up with a middle-frequency signal to aid in location of an exit.[20]

Proportion can improve visibility. Letters and numbers should have a width-to-height ratio between 1:1 and 3:5. The letter X, for example, could be 3 by 5 in. The ratio of the stroke width to the height should be between 1:5 and 1:10. If each line used to make the X is 1 in wide, then the letter itself could be between 5 and 10 in high.[21]

Signs should be mounted at a height between 54 and 66 in.[22] Signs for children should be no higher than 40 in.[23] An entry sign should be located on the wall nearest the door latch. Signs should also be placed to avoid glare from windows and light sources, and glare-free materials should be selected.

PLANTS

Plants add a feeling of life and growth to a space. They absorb carbon dioxide and other unwanted gases while adding oxygen to the air. People with allergies, for example, can use Ficus plants to absorb formaldehyde, which outgasses from many building materials and carpeting. (Fig. 7-32)

In a large planter keep houseplants in smaller pots so that they can be easily moved. Larger potted plants can be moved with a mobile plant stand. (Fig. 7-33)

CHEMICALS REMOVED BY HOUSEHOLD PLANTS FROM A SEALED EXPERIMENTAL CHAMBER DURING A 24-HOUR EXPOSURE PERIOD

	Formaldehyde			Benzene			Trichloroethylene		
	Initial (p/m)	Final (p/m)	Percent Removed	Initial (p/m)	Final (p/m)	Percent Removed	Initial (p/m)	Final (p/m)	Percent Removed
Mass cane	20	6	70	14	11	21.4	16	14	12.5
Pot mum	18	7	61	58	27	53	17	10	41.2
Gerbera daisy	16	8	50	65	21	67.7	20	13	35
Warneckei	8	4	50	27	13	52	20	18	10
Ficus	19	10	47.4	20	14	30	19	17	10.5
Leak control	18	17.5	2.8	20	19	5	20	18	10

Note: Plants were maintained in a commercial-type greenhouse until ready for testing. Each test, 24-h in duration, was conducted in a sealed chamber with temperature and light intensity of 30 0C +-1 and 125 footcandles +- 5, respectively.

7-32

7-33

LAMPS

Avoid installing any projecting wall lamp that could be an obstacle to a wheelchair. Floor lamps can be moved out of the way and can be easily positioned from a wheelchair for task lighting. Specify adjustable height floor lamps with touch controls. (Fig. 7-34)

Keep lamps at each task location. The lamps should have heavily weighted bases for stability. Squeeze switches on cords are easy for many people to operate. A touch converter eliminates the switch. Touch the metal surface on the lamp to turn it on. (Fig. 7-35)

Choose designs that can be used in both the living room and bedroom for added flexibility. (Fig. 7-36) Use translucent shades for reading and opaque shades for accent color and ambient lighting. Plastic shades and fixtures are prone to volatile outgassing when exposed to high lamp temperatures. These gases may cause problems for people with allergies.[24]

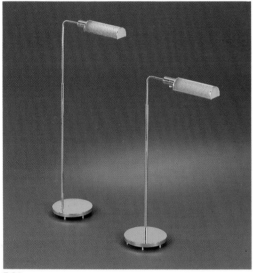

7-34

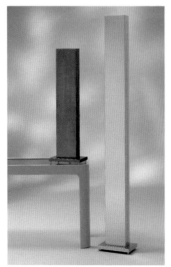

7-35

7-36

BEDROOM ACCESSORIES

U Save energy, exertion, and time with well-organized storage. Plan "a place for everything" so that effort will not be wasted looking for lost items. Expand reachable storage in the closet with hanging racks for shoes and sweaters. Keep closet shelves transparent above eye level with plastic or wire shelves. (Fig. 7-37) Save space at a reachable level with racks and shelves attached to the backs of doors. Add a carousel system that rotates hanging clothes. This type of system is appropriate for clients in wheelchairs or anyone needing access to a tight storage space. Clothing that becomes lodged behind the system, however, will be difficult to retrieve from a wheelchair. (Fig. 7-38)

U Accessories like keys, staplers, scissors, paper clips, tape, eyeglasses, pencils, and pens can be placed in a variety of locations to save the energy required for extra trips and prolonged searches. Specify accessory holders at multiple locations. Have a pad and pencil at each telephone together with a directory.

7-37

7-38

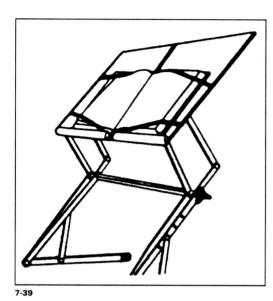

7-39

U Provide a lap stand for reading or working in bed. (Fig. 7-39) Bands on the stand hold the book firmly in place and allow the pages to be turned with one hand. For ease of bed making with one hand, specify a quilt with a blanket cover that replaces the bedspread, blanket, and top sheet. With a covered comforter, the bed can be made with one easy motion. Also, a short comforter is easier to manipulate than a bedspread extending to the floor.

For people who have trouble turning over in bed, suggest satin sheets which are used with satin pajamas. (Fig. 7-40) People in pain can move more easily on satin sheets; some maintain that this is the only way they can sleep. Others slip out of bed or have difficulty getting into bed.

7-40

8. Kitchens

Flexibility is the key to successful universal kitchen design. At least one counter in the kitchen should be adjustable so that it can be lowered to meet the needs of future residents. Removable cabinets will also make the home easier to sell by appealing to a larger market, including people in wheelchairs and people who need to sit down to cook or wash the dishes. (Fig. 8-1)

A basic work triangle is a universal concept that should be planned between the sink, range, and refrigerator. Because many people with strength differences must slide pans between the sink and stove, it is helpful if the sink and range are on the same level and connected by a continuous counter.

Remodeling a kitchen for wheelchair accessibility is costly now and may be costly again in the future when the home is resold or rented to a limited market of people in wheelchairs. The "alternate kitchen" is an idea of universal interest that can increase the resale value of the home. With this plan, the existing kitchen counters remain at a height for standing users, while a second kitchen is temporarily installed for wheelchair use. When the primary kitchen is accessible, the alternate kitchen may be planned for a standing user. A breakfast nook, dining room, or utility room could have hot and cold water lines and a drain concealed during construction, so that the alternate kitchen can be added at a later date with minimal expense. (Fig. 8-2) This feature alone may increase the resale value of the home. The kitchen could be wheelchair accessible without the stigma of "handicapped housing."

The alternate kitchen concept is also useful to anyone with a temporary injury or a house guest in a wheelchair. If elderly parents need family assistance, for example, a temporary kitchen could be installed for wheelchair use with minimal expense using a portable refrigerator, a two-burner hot plate, and a toaster oven or microwave.

8-1

CABINETS

When using removable cabinets, be sure the counter is adjustable, not attached to the base cabinets. A custom cabinet should be finished on both exterior sides to allow flexibility in future use. It can be designed as a freestanding unit that is totally removable, as a unit that folds up in place, or as a unit with a removable front and base. (Figure 8-3) Cabinet height is a primary consideration for wheelchair access. Base cabinets should be adjustable to allow a minimum clearance (27 in) between the floor and the underside of the counter. A clear kick space (8¾ in high by 6 in deep)[1] should be left between the floor and the cabinets to protect them from wheelchair abrasions and to allow a closer approach. For people with sufficient mobility, drawers can be recessed into the toe space to store items that are seldom used.

Install upper cabinets on heavy-duty commercial shelf brackets between counter height and the high reach limit. (Fig. 8-4) Cabinets that lower with the push of a button are also appropriate. (Fig. 8-5) An open shelf between a cabinet and the counter will increase reachable storage space. (Fig. 8-6)

Kitchen space planning is essential for wheelchair use. A clear floor space of 30 by 48 in should be allowed for each work area in a triangle created by the refrigerator, range, and sink. This space allowance is also helpful for people who use mobility aids.

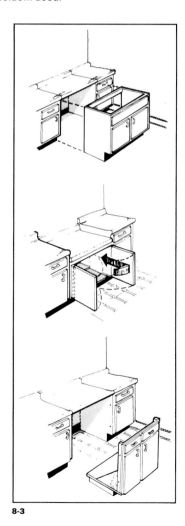

8-3

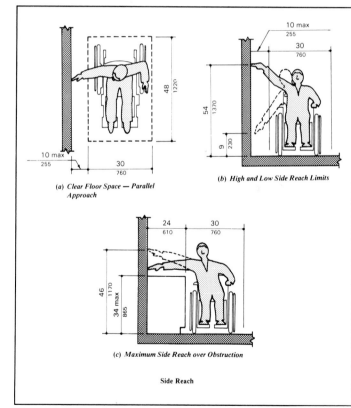

(a) Clear Floor Space — Parallel Approach

(b) High and Low Side Reach Limits

(c) Maximum Side Reach over Obstruction

Side Reach

8-4

8-5

8-6

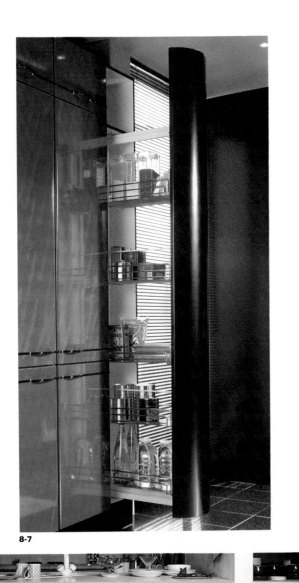

8-7

(U) One of the most convenient plans incorporating these clear floor spaces is an L-shaped kitchen with a level counter space extending between the refrigerator and the wall oven. Clear knee space should be provided under the entire counter, including the sink. The counter and sink should be adjustable (between 28 and 36 in).

(U) Plan a breakfast area close to the kitchen counter to shorten the distance for serving and clearing. Storage between kitchen and dining room should open from both sides. (Fig. 8-7) This is particularly helpful with corner cabinets, where back storage space may be out of reach from one side.

(U) A movable cabinet under the sink can serve as a cart between the counter and the table. When the cabinet is moved out, the space under the counter is clear for wheelchair access and the top of the cart can serve as extra counter space. The cabinet can also serve as a refuse container or be used to hold other large items that are difficult to remove from the back of the other cabinets. The cabinet should have casters (Fig. 8-8) and a top rail to prevent items from sliding off.

Prefabricated cabinets (36 in high) designed for wall-mounting may be usable, depending on the height of the client. Eliminate the 3-in toe space and lower the cabinets to the floor. This method sacrifices clearance for wheelchair footrests but saves the expense of custom work. When using this method, leave enough clearance for the doors to swing open over the kitchen floor covering.

To access the sink under existing cabinets, cut a large semicircle out of the cabinet floor to provide a space for footrests. Remove the center stile and attach it to one of the door edges.

8-8

Kitchen Storage Details

U Plan extra storage space in the kitchen to eliminate clutter and to cut down on the number of needed shopping trips. Uncluttered space is a boon for everyone, but especially for the elderly, people with vision and mobility differences, and individuals with concentration problems.

U Suggest organizing items by activity; keep the coffee, coffeepot, and filters in the same area. Store baking equipment and ingredients in the same cabinet close to the oven. Keep frequently used items at the front of cabinets and heavier items on lower shelves; eliminate items that are seldom used. Use dividers in drawers to organize utensils and kitchen gadgets. A system of this type is especially important for blind people. (Fig. 8-9)

U Use high cabinets to store seasonal items and seldom-used equipment. Install clear plastic shelves or metal racks on upper cabinets to allow easy viewing. For people who are allergic to petrochemicals, use mesh shelves installed in metal or hardwood cabinets. (Fig. 8-10)[2]

8-9

8-10

8-11

U A wire rack can be added to the back of a cabinet door. (Fig. 8-11) For additional storage, a built-in waste bin with automatic lid can be attached to a cabinet door. (Fig. 8-12) Even the space between the cabinet door and sink can be utilized.

U Dispensers can help bring cans and bottles within reach. Lazy susans or slide-out rotary shelves also improve access. (Fig. 8-13) Half-circled pull-out shelves are particularly useful in corners. (Fig. 8-14)

8-12

8-13

8-15

8-16

U Shelves attached to cabinet doors help to bring storage within reach. These shelves must have rims to keep objects from sliding off. Roll-out shelves also need rims. (Fig. 8-15)

U Removable bins offer access and flexibility on any shelf. Bins and heavy objects slide more easily on a shelf with a smooth surface. For faster access, plan shallow shelves rather than deeper kitchen cabinets. (Fig. 8-16) Reaching into deep base cabinets can be particularly difficult. Plan a pantry in the space between studs in the wall to add shallow shelving. (Fig. 8-17)

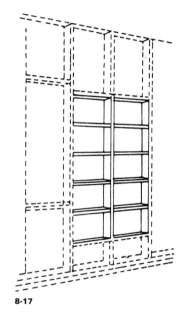

8-17

Kitchen Drawers

U A pull-out pantry can be installed in minimal cabinet space. (Fig. 8-18) A pull-out drawer for pans is also a convenience. (Fig. 8-19)

U Drawers should be equipped with full extension roller-type slides, which will allow access to deep storage. (Fig. 8-20) Pull-out drawers should have one lower side to allow access from a seated position. (Fig. 8-21)

8-18

8-20

8-19

8-21

Kitchen Cabinet Doors

U Most cabinets now incorporate hinges that hold the door closed but require more strength to open than touch latches. With a touch latch, the door opens with a push rather than a pull. Magnetic catches on cabinets may be difficult to open unless they are combined with touch latches. (Fig. 8-22)

U Cabinets with handles should have extra-long C pulls. (Fig. 8-23) Mount handles vertically on upper cabinets as close to the bottom of the doors as possible. On base cabinets, mount the pulls near the top edge of the cabinet doors.

For people with vision differences, choose flat door handles that can can be marked in braille. Alphabetize spices in a rack and label them in braille. Mount the rack on the inside of a cabinet or pantry door for easy use. (Fig. 8-24)

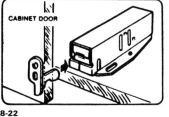

8-22

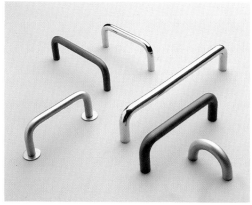

8-23

8-24

For people with mobility differences who may need to lean on cabinets for support, use systems that require no pulls or knobs. (Fig. 8-25) If hardware is included, test it for strength and durability. Knobs should not protrude more than 1/8 in.[3] Use a slightly textured finish on the cabinet to prevent slipping.

Sliding kitchen cabinet doors may be easier to operate from a wheelchair than doors that swing out. Tambour doors won't block other storage areas when open. Display items can be stored in open cabinets.

Because open upper cabinet doors cannot be detected by blind people who use canes, install bi-fold or sliding cabinet doors to prevent injury. Specify automatic door closing hinges on swinging cabinet doors that do not need to remain open.

8-25

KITCHEN COUNTERS

U Three steps are often repeated in the kitchen during food preparation. First, the food is removed from the cupboard or refrigerator and often washed in the sink. Next, the food is mixed. Finally, it is cooked. For this reason, the sink should be located between the stove and the refrigerator, with counter space on both sides of the sink (18 in minimum).

U People with vision differences use counters to line up all the ingredients and utensils in logical order for the task. For this purpose, the countertop should be at least 4 ft long. People who stand on crutches or in a walker also appreciate longer clear counters to provide adequate body support. Deaf people need extra counter space to set things down, freeing their hands for sign language.[4] People in wheelchairs have an awkward angle for lifting objects onto counters. Unbroken counter spaces allow objects to be pulled or pushed instead.

U Kitchens or work areas should have a minimum clear floor space of 40 in between opposite counters or walls for wheelchair use if the kitchen is open on both ends.[5] For a U-turn in a wheelchair, the clear floor space should be 5 ft in diameter.[6] Three-wheelers may require a slightly larger area for a smooth turn. (Fig. 8-26)

Counter Heights

U Counter surfaces at a variety of heights allow people of all ages, sizes, and abilities to work comfortably. Adjustable counters, pull-out breadboards, or multiple-height tables should be considered. (Fig. 8-27)

78 min
1985

60 min
1525

8-26

8-27

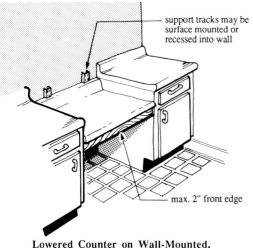

support tracks may be
surface mounted or
recessed into wall

— max. 2" front edge

8-28   Lowered Counter on Wall-Mounted,
Adjustable Support Brackets

**Convenient Heights of
Work Surfaces for Seated People***

Conditions of Use	Short Women		Tall Men	
	in	mm	in	mm
Seated in a wheelchair:				
Manual work:				
Desk or removable armrests	26	660	30	760
Fixed, full-size armrests†	32‡	815	32‡	815
Light, detailed work:				
Desk or removable armrests	29	735	34	865
Fixed, full-size armrests†	32‡	815	34	865
Seated in a 16-in (405-mm) ·high chair:				
Manual work	26	660	27	685
Light, detailed work	28	710	31	785

*All dimensions are based on a work-surface thickness of
1·1/2 in (38 mm) and a clearance of 1·1/2 in (38 mm)
between legs and the underside of a work surface.

† This type of wheelchair arm does not interfere with the
positioning of a wheelchair under a work surface.

‡ This dimension is limited by the height of the armrests: a
lower height would be preferable. Some people in this group
prefer lower work surfaces, which require positioning the
wheelchair back from the edge of the counter.

8-29

Ⓤ Adjustable surfaces offer flexibility for people with strength and coordination differences. Counters can be mounted on recessed heavy-duty shelf standards screwed into studs or solid blocking.[7] If only one adjustable height counter is installed, place it next to the refrigerator. This will improve reach into the refrigerator for people in wheelchairs and minimize the inconvenience of counters staggered at different heights. Specify a finish on adjacent counter ends and cabinets since these will be exposed when the counter is lowered.

Ⓤ Adjustable counters can be lowered for use by children and future residents. Taller people may prefer counters up to 42 in high for some tasks. The minimum clearance required for wheelchair access is 27 in. A counter no more than 2 in thick allows a client in a wheelchair to work comfortably. (Fig. 8-28) If the counter has a skirtboard, recess it a minimum of 12 in from the front edge.[8]

Ⓤ A counter lowered for wheelchair access may be at a supportive height for a standing person to knead dough or perform other heavy manual work. The ideal height for this work is calculated to be about 10 in below elbow height (from a standing position).[9] Writing and light work can best be done on a work surface 1 to 3 in below elbow height when standing. When seated, light work surfaces should be slightly higher than manual work surfaces. (Fig. 8-29) With limited counter space, consider a motor-driven countertop that can be changed in height for a variety of tasks. (Fig. 8-30)

8-30

8-31

8-32

Counter Finishes

U Specify a heat-resistant counter next to the cooktop to prevent burns. Ceramic tile is a good choice, but it is more difficult to slide pans over tile joints than over a smooth surface. Many people need to slide heavy pans between the range and the sink. Smooth, heat-resistant synthetic counters are available for this purpose.

U Surface burns, scratches, and cuts can be removed from solid synthetics with a light sanding. Matching sinks can be fabricated with angled sides and in custom depths to improve access. These tops are also preferable for people who are allergic to laminate tops adhered to chemically offensive substrates. (Fig. 8-31)

U A slight texture or pattern on the counter will conceal water spots and scratches, but too much texture (like deep leather grains) will hold dirt. Colors that are too light or too dark will show smudge and grease marks. (Fig. 8-32)

8-33

8-34

Details

Ⓤ Corners are often difficult to reach from a wheelchair. An L-shaped counter design has only one corner, but a person who uses the counter for support may have trouble leaning into it. Add a straightedge to the corner of the kitchen counter for better support and more work space. (Fig. 8-33)

Ⓤ Because a person in a wheelchair must rest his or her arms on the edge of the counter while working, bevel or round the edge for comfort. (Fig. 8-34) This will also protect those who may fall against the counter. Elevated rolled edges prevent spills but make it difficult to work directly on the counter from a wheelchair. Rolling out a pie crust, for example, is almost impossible on an elevated edge. Slope the counter slightly to drain toward the sink. This slope also helps people slide heavy pots from the work area to the sink.[10]

Ⓤ Add a rail to the edge of the counter as a safety feature since many accidents occur in the kitchen. The rail also protects the counter from chipping and can be used to pull up to the counter in a wheelchair. (Fig. 8-35)

8-35

Alternatives to Counters

A fold-down work surface can be added to increase counter space without taking up floor space for wheelchair use. Self-folding or rising work surfaces should be specified for people who have difficulty with reach. (Fig. 8-36) Additional fold-down shelves could be located under the counter to increase storage without creating a problem for wheelchair access. A sliding shelf over the counter can greatly increase work space.

Extra counter space can also be created by replacing a drawer with a pull-out work surface. If a lower counter height is required for stirring, cut a hole in the surface to hold the mixing bowl. Line the hole with a rubber strip to keep the bowl from slipping. (Fig. 8-37)

A movable chopping board over the sink can increase usable counter space. Choose one with a vegetable basket on the side for drainage. Acrylic boards can be cleaned more easily and completely than wood, but wood boards can be customized for one-handed use. Nails can be driven into the wood to impale vegetables so they can be peeled with one hand. A raised edge can be added to one corner to help hold bread in place when buttering. (Fig. 8-38) A potato peeler can be clamped on for one-handed use.

8-36

8-37

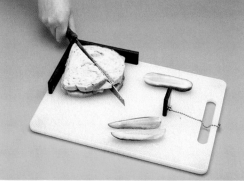

8-38

FIXTURES AND APPLIANCES

Choose labor-saving devices like self-cleaning ovens, frost-free refrigerators, and microwave ovens. Pans and utensils do not get as hot in a microwave, a safety feature that is especially important for people with reduced sensation, providing they take care to avoid steam burns when opening a container. People with vision differences can also appreciate the safety of a microwave, since no flames are involved.

Ice dispensers may be especially critical for people who have trouble using ice trays. Door-mounted models bring ice within reach and are helpful for people who have the strength and coordination to use them. Before purchasing, make sure that these features can be plumbed into a water supply.

Controls

Make sure switches are accompanied by warning lights to show that appliances are on. Redundant cuing like this makes controls more noticeable by all people. Controls should also be large and easy to read.

Choose an appliance with controls and accessories on the side or front, not in the back. (Fig. 8-39) Built-in appliances should have controls at counter level. Outlets and switches can be located on the fascia of the countertop for easier reach, but this location will also be more accessible to children. It may be helpful to include automatic turn-off switches on appliances.

Some appliances may need an electrical outlet under the counter. Mount an electric can opener on the inside of a lower cabinet door. Store a mixer on a pop-up shelf under the counter. To operate other appliances, permanently install a motor base on the countertop for stability. Many appliances, including food processors, can be operated with one hand from a permanently installed motor base. (Fig. 8-40) Locate the motor between the cooktop and the sink, where most food preparation will take place.

8-39

8-40

For clients with strength and coordination differences, specify push bars rather than pull-out buttons, touch controls (Fig. 8-41) rather than dials, and controls that can be operated with the palms up, not down. Test a control to see if it can be operated with a closed fist. Where greatest accuracy is required, hand and arm motion should be used rather than foot and leg movements. The hand should be held close to the body at approximately elbow level to maximize accuracy.

Avoid controls that can be activated accidentally. Although touch controls are the easiest to use, they are also easier to turn on by accident. Remember that touch controls can also be easily used by children.

Specify controls that do not require sustained effort. Some push-type faucets, for example, require sustained holding to operate. Also, keep in mind that it is easier to operate controls in front of the body rather than at the side.

Faucets

A faucet with a single lever can be operated with one hand. Paddles, blades, or push-type mechanisms are easier to use than knobs and are good choices for people who may be confused by single-lever controls. Many faucet controls can be mounted on the front apron of the counter for an easier approach from a wheelchair.

8-41

To eliminate controls, consider a faucet that incorporates an infrared sensor to control water flow. (Fig. 8-42) A faucet with a spring-loaded push knob or push rod can be operated with the palm of one hand. The rod attaches to the faucet and is operated by pressure from a cup or glass. A gooseneck faucet can be used to fill a pan on the counter without lifting the pan into the sink. (Fig. 8-43)

One innovative faucet design combines a gooseneck style with a pull-out spray on a retractable hose. Both the faucet and the spray can be installed in an existing sink with a single hole. (Fig. 8-44)

Faucet controls should be located uniformly on all sinks throughout the home to prevent accidental scalding. Hot water taps are normally on the left, cold on the right. Red and blue color coding can be used to differentiate hot and cold taps, respectively. (Fig. 8-45)

8-42

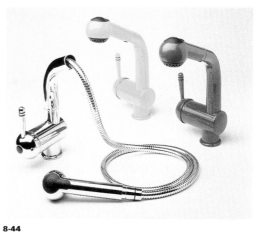

8-44

8-45

8-43

Sinks

Wheelchair access to a sink can be improved by the placement of the drain control, the depth of the sink, and the location of the installation. The drain control may be located on the countertop to improve reach. (Fig. 8-46) The sink should be no deeper than 6½ in.[11] If an existing sink is deeper, recess the front of the countertop for a closer approach. From a wheelchair, the client should be able to place one hand flat on the bottom of the sink. A removable rack can also be used to improve reach. (Fig. 8-47)

Consider installing two sinks in the kitchen, one at the correct height for the cook, the other for the rest of the family. If the cook is standing with arms relaxed, the bottom of the sink should be 2 in higher than wrist height.[12] If the main sink is not accessible, add a bar sink on a lowered counter. (Fig. 8-48) This sink will also be accessible to children.

Specify a sink with the drain to the back and to one side so that connecting pipes will be either to the left or right, not in the center, allowing a closer wheelchair approach. With a double sink, only one side needs to be accessible.

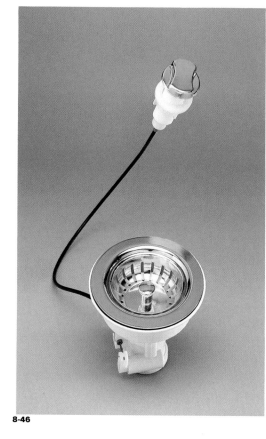

8-46

8-47

8-48

8-49

It's easier to ease pots and pans out of a sink with angled sides. A stainless sink is thinner and allows more knee clearance than a porcelain sink. Also, it doesn't chip, an advantage for people with differences in coordination.

Adjustable-height sinks are available in prefabricated models with manual or automatic controls. (Fig. 8-49) When customizing an installation, simply change the tailpiece to alter the height. To do so, a flexible supply line must be in place and the trap must be low enough to receive the tailpiece at the lowest position of the sink. (Fig. 8-50)

Insulate the pipes to prevent burns, or add a nonmetallic panel that can be removed for maintenance. The cover also keeps the pipes out of sight. (Fig. 8-51)

Ovens

Specify wall-mounted ovens instead of floor models. Wall ovens are easier for all people, but are critical to wheelchair use. Install drawers under the oven for convenient storage. Above the oven, add a cabinet with vertical dividers for baking pans, broilers, trays, and lids.

Ovens mounted above shoulder level are often unusable from a wheelchair, since it is difficult to lower heavy pots and pans with arms extended above shoulder height. For increased lifting ability, the arms should be bent at a right angle, not extended above the shoulder. Mount the oven door just above lap height and insulate both sides of the oven to prevent burns.

It's easier to reach into the back of an oven with a side-hinged door. (Fig. 8-52) Plan the door latch and controls on the side next to the open counter.

Install a shelf under the side-hinged door to hold a heavy pan after it is removed from the oven. The shelf should pull out to a minimum of 10 in.[13]

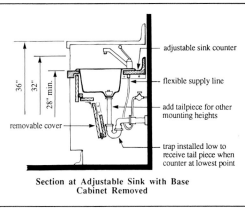

adjustable sink counter

flexible supply line

add tailpiece for other mounting heights

removable cover

36"
32"
28" min.

trap installed low to receive tail piece when counter at lowest point

Section at Adjustable Sink with Base Cabinet Removed

8-50

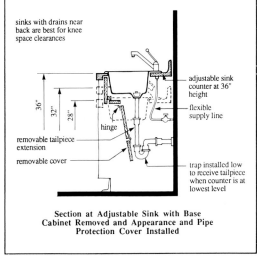

sinks with drains near back are best for knee space clearances

adjustable sink counter at 36" height

flexible supply line

hinge

removable tailpiece extension

removable cover

36"
32"
28"

trap installed low to receive tailpiece when counter is at lowest level

Section at Adjustable Sink with Base Cabinet Removed and Appearance and Pipe Protection Cover Installed

8-51

Next to the oven, plan an accessible counter with knee space. This space can be used to reach fully into the oven, which is necessary for maintaining a model that is not self-cleaning. (Fig. 8-53)

For people with vision differences, install wall ovens with controls at eye level. Microwaves may be safer to use since there is no flame or hot element involved. Specify a model with visual, tactile, and audible controls.

Ranges

Cooking is easier with wheelchair space below a cooktop, but the danger of accidental burns caused by spills increases. Raised heating elements should be avoided; it is easier to tip a pan off an elevated surface. To prevent burns, electrical shocks, and abrasions, insulate surfaces under and on both sides of the range.

Magnetic induction cooktops are more expensive, but they greatly reduce the danger of burns and fire. They eliminate hot elements and offer more stability for pots and pans. Some models chime when a pan is lifted from the surface. (Fig. 8-54) Install magnetic induction cooktops level with counters.

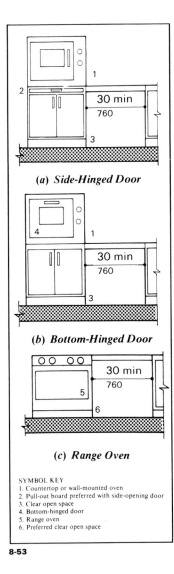

(a) Side-Hinged Door

(b) Bottom-Hinged Door

(c) Range Oven

SYMBOL KEY
1. Countertop or wall-mounted oven
2. Pull-out board preferred with side-opening door
3. Clear open space
4. Bottom-hinged door
5. Range oven
6. Preferred clear open space

8-53

8-54

Wheelchair clearance can be allowed under the range by planning an open knee space or by specifying a range that pulls out. With this type of unit, storage is not sacrificed to knee space. Make sure that a clear floor space of 30 by 48 in is maintained when the range is open.

It may not be necessary to provide clearance under the cooktop for wheelchair use if cooking elements and controls are in line along the front of the counter. Controls mounted on the fascia of the counter, however, may be too accessible to children.

As an alternative, to prevent burns, stagger back elements so that they are accessible without reaching over a front element. (Fig. 8-55) Do not plan storage in a cabinet over the cooktop.

A small wall-mounted mirror can be used to monitor pots on back burners. The mirror eliminates the need to reach over a hot element to check the food. Make sure the mirror is removable for easy maintenance.

Wall-mount exhaust fan controls, or use a fan mounted on the counter with controls within reach. (Fig. 8-56) Down-draft fans generate less ambient noise than updraft models, an advantage to people with differences in hearing. Vent the fan outdoors for more efficient control of smoke and odors.

For people who depend on the sense of touch, install guardrails around gas burners and electric elements. Gas offers auditory and olfactory cues as well as visible flames. Specify an electric range, however, if the client is unable to smell gas or is hypersensitive to gas odors.

8-55

8-56

Refrigerators

8-57

A side-by-side refrigerator allows greater access from a wheelchair, but it is difficult to wheel around two swinging doors. This refrigerator is often wider than a conventional model and may take up too much space. If space if limited, use a refrigerator with the freezer below. (Fig. 8-57) Install the handle side toward the sink.

Plan an accessible space under the counter next to the refrigerator. Make sure the refrigerator door can swing back 180° to allow maximum access, which is especially important for cleaning or defrosting. A shallow horizontal refrigerator with a top door can be mounted on a countertop with wheelchair clearance underneath. A number of these smaller units can be distributed around the kitchen and throughout the house where needed. (Fig. 8-58)

8-58

U Small details on a refrigerator can make a big difference, especially for wheelchair use. Make sure the controls are toward the front of the unit. Look for stops on shelves; swing-out adjustable shelves are an option. Permanent shelves should not be deeper than 13 in. If the shelves are too deep, use lazy susans.

Refrigerators with magnetic door catches require less strength to open than those with latches, but sometimes even the magnetic seal is too difficult. As a temporary measure, a portion of the seal can be blocked with tape or a plastic clip. Also try a looped strap over the handle for people with reduced strength.

U Extra shelves, especially in the freezer section, will make it easier to reach more items without moving others. Adjustable door shelves can hold gallon-size containers and larger bottles, putting these heavy items in the most accessible location. (Fig. 8-59) Two small crispers in the refrigerator are easier to handle than one large unit. Specify crispers on roller guides.

U It is often difficult to reach the bottom of a chest freezer, especially from a wheelchair. Specify an upright model and use lazy susans for items in the back.

Dishwashers

Specify a dishwasher with a recessed motor so that the toe space can be elevated to clear wheelchair footrests. Front-loading dishwashers with side-hinged doors allow closer wheelchair access. If space is available, provide access on both sides of a front-loading washer, and slightly elevate the unit. (Fig. 8-60) All of the rack space should be accessible from the front of the machine. The silverware basket should be on the door and equipped with a handle.

8-59

8-60

Portable top-loading dishwashers and their sink attachments are difficult for many people to use. Specify front-loading dishwashers with porcelain or plastic interiors; stainless steel interiors may become too hot. (Fig. 8-61)

Redundant cuing should be specified on the dishwasher. People with hearing impairments especially appreciate a visual off and on indicator. Quiet dishwashers are also available to reduce the ambient noise in the kitchen.

Garbage Disposals

In considering a garbage disposal, remember that the disposal will use knee space under the sink but will save frequent trips to empty the garbage outdoors. (Fig. 8-62) Maintain wheelchair clearance under a garbage disposal by selecting a model without sound insulation. The unit should be installed under an accessible sink with the drain to the back and side.

A garbage disposal can also be installed on the deep side of a double sink, leaving knee space below the other side for wheelchair access. A continuous-feed model with a separate switch will be easier to control than a batch-feed model with the switch in the drain.

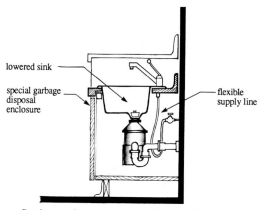

lowered sink

special garbage disposal enclosure

flexible supply line

Section at Special Garbage Disposal Enclosure
8-62

8-61

Trash Compactors

Although trash compactors also save trips to empty the garbage, the compacted bag may be too heavy to handle. For people in wheelchairs, the compactor takes up valuable space under the counter.

Hot Water Dispensers

Hot water dispensers eliminate the need to heat, carry or pour boiling water. Specify a model equipped with a lever. (Fig. 8-63)

Small Appliances

Select small appliances on the basis of weight, balance, and control. Specify rechargeable models to avoid the limits of a cord.

A cordless electric carving knife is usually easier to use than a regular knife. A cordless scrubber is helpful for people who have trouble exerting enough pressure to clean pots and pans. A mixer can be too heavy for many people to lift; look for a lightweight model. The mixer should have good balance, an upright rest, and controls that can be operated with one hand.

Recess small appliance cabinets in the splash at counter level for extra work space. The appliances can then be moved out on the counter without lifting. To save counter space, a microwave oven, toaster, coffee maker, or other appliance can be suspended from the cabinet above or used from a pull-out cart. (Fig. 8-64) The cart can also be moved to the dining area, allowing use of appliances at the table.

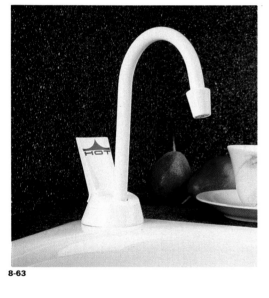

8-63

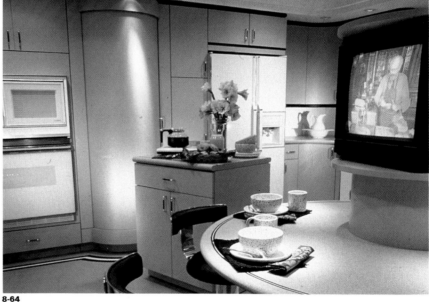

8-64

U Because a conventional toaster can be difficult to use, choose a toaster oven, which requires less dexterity.

U Some small kitchen appliances offer user-friendly controls; the C grips and paddle controls on many food processors are good examples. Also appropriate are electric frying pans available with braille dials and large baffled controls. (Fig. 8-65) Such pans are designed for stability and are available with two handles for people with reduced strength.

U An electric can opener that requires sustained squeezing for operation can be too difficult for clients with strength or coordination differences to use; for safety's sake, choose a one-handed model that locks in the on position. (Fig. 8-66) Beaters are also available for use with one hand. (Fig. 8-67)

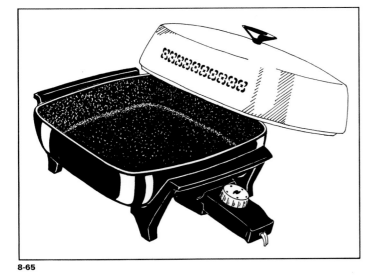

8-65

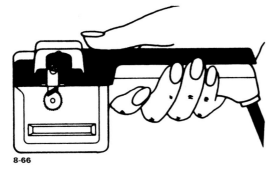

8-66

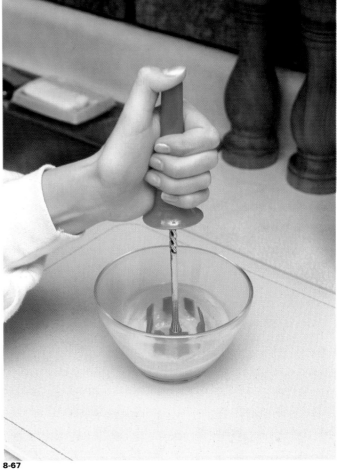

8-67

8-68

KITCHEN ACCESSORIES

Utensils

U To keep utensils within reach from a wheelchair, consider installing pegs or wall-mounted racks between the counters and cabinets. (Fig. 8-68) Slanting pegs are easier to use than hooks, which can catch on pan handles. Utensils can also be stored in hanging baskets.

U Many items are designed for one-handed use. A breadboard and knife set is available to help in slicing. (Fig. 8-69) A rotary recipe file, for example, can be mounted on the inside of a cabinet door to keep recipes reachable yet off the counter. Another example of a one-handed utensil is a pizza cutter, which can also be used to cut meat, bread, and vegetables.

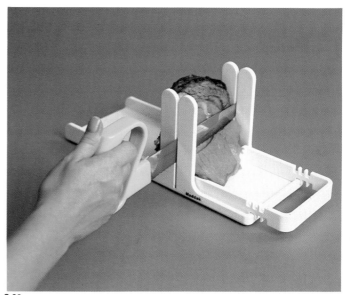

8-69

Cookware

 Glass pots and pans, because they are see-through, allow people in wheelchairs to monitor cooking food. Glass cookware can be used to cook, store, and serve food, reducing the number of cooking items needed. Choose lightweight cookware for people with strength differences and heavier sets for clients with tremors. Pans with double handles are easier to lift.

Dining Accessories

 For increased grip strength, choose smaller drinking glasses. Use larger glasses for clients who have trouble tilting their heads; two-handled cups may be easier to hold. For increased coordination, select cups with large handles and dinner plates with deeper sides to help in scooping the food onto the spoon. (Fig. 8-70) Although heavier dishes, like stoneware, retain heat better, they are usually more difficult to lift.

For people with coordination difficulties, sectioned plates make eating easier. (Fig. 8-71)

 Silverware with pistol grips or handles that conform to the hand improve grip strength. To improve strength in slicing, consider a knife which operates with a rocking motion instead of a slicing motion. (Fig. 8-72)

 For people with vision differences, be sure dishes contrast with tablecloths. Specify plates with borders so that the edges of plates can be more easily seen.

8-70

8-71

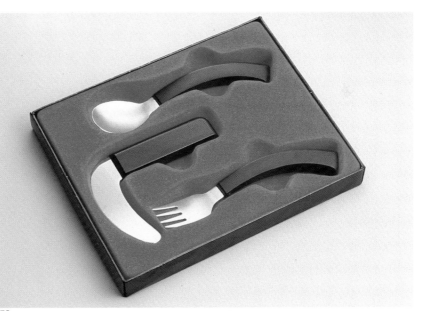

8-72

Kitchen Maintenance Accessories

(U) Everyday products can be used to enhance a variety of different abilities. For people with reduced grip strength, for instance, trays can be used to clear tables so dishes do not have to be carried separately. To clean up spills, pails of water can be moved more easily on caster frames. A sponge mop with a wringer mechanism requires less strength and coordination than a cloth mop. A dustpan with a long handle requires less bending, and a feather duster with a telescoping handle increases reach. A wastebasket with a nonslip foot control can be opened without the use of hands.

Accessories for Kitchen Safety

(U) Every kitchen should be equipped with a fire extinguisher. Specify a model with a sodium bicarbonate base to combat grease fires.

(U) Because people with reduced sensation cannot easily feel burns, select cookware with handles that don't become hot. Also, suggest oven-proof mittens, which are easier to use than potholders. Insulated rubber gloves can improve grip strength on dishes while protecting hands from hot, irritating dishwater.

9. Bathrooms and Utility Spaces

In public rest rooms, wheelchair-accessible spaces are convenient for many users. These larger stalls offer travelers enough room to roll in luggage or strollers. Parents have enough space to help children, and people using crutches and walkers have more room to maneuver. A recent trend has been to increase the size of accessible stalls to 5 by 5 ft and to include individual sinks in the stalls.

Residential bathrooms must be safe, convenient, and adaptable to a variety of different abilities. With a few initial considerations, baths can be adapted to wheelchair use at a later date. Plan removable cabinets, adjustable counters, an accessible shower, and reinforced sidewalls. Walls can be reinforced with $3/4$-in plywood or with wood blocking installed between the studs. This inexpensive reinforcement will provide for installation of the grab bars, sink, towel bars, and shower seat.

SHOWERS

Shower Enclosures

A shower is quicker, easier, and safer to use than a bathtub. After one transfer from the wheelchair to the shower wheelchair, the user can roll into the shower, under the sink, or over a toilet without additional transfer. The wheel-in shower can be installed in the enclosure space of a bathtub (30 in by 60 in). This elongated shower design provides more maneuvering space than a standard square shower. (Fig. 9-1) It should be equipped with a hand-held shower system and with temperature and surge controls to provide a safe flow of water.

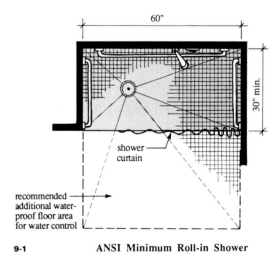

9-1 ANSI Minimum Roll-in Shower

U This enclosure can also be planned in a square or round design. (Fig. 9-2) A corner shower ramped on two sides allows access from more than one direction. (Fig. 9-3)

U The shower floor should be sloped rather than curbed, since a curb could be a tripping hazard. The best method, however, is to gradually slope the entire bathroom floor to drain into the shower. A steep slope makes it difficult to maneuver a shower wheelchair. Be sure to specify nonslip tiling. (Fig. 9-4)

Water can also be contained by recessing the floor of a wheel-in shower. Use a grating to raise the floor height to that of the bathroom. If recessed or sloping floors are not practical, plan a slight ramp up to the grating. A grating and ramp can also be used to access an existing shower with a lip.

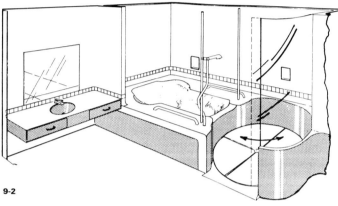

9-2

9-3

9-4

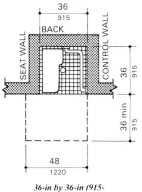

A square shower takes up less space than a bathtub (as little as 3 by 3 ft), but it requires a shower seat and cannot be used easily with a wheelchair. The dimensions of this shower are critical so that grab bars, shower controls, and accessories are within reach.[1] (Fig. 9-5)

This smaller shower will require a ½-in curb to contain water.[2] During transfer to a shower seat, the front wheels of a wheelchair are placed over the curb to prevent the chair from sliding backward. Shower controls should be mounted on the wall opposite the seat.

Specify a fold-up shower seat to clear the space for standing users. (Fig. 9-6) Choose a vinyl seat slatted for drainage. (Fig. 9-7) Make sure the corners are rounded and the back, if any, is wood or textured vinyl.

36-in by 36-in (915-mm by 915-mm) Stall

9-5   Shower Sizes and Clearances

9-6

9-7

9-8

U The shower stall should have rounded corners for ease of maintenance, and the floor should be slip-resistant. (Fig. 9-8) Plan showers with curtains, not doors. (Fig. 9-9) Curtains on showers without curbs should be longer than floor length to prevent water from escaping. Ceiling-mounted shower curtains have a cleaner appearance, especially when they curve around two sides of the shower.

A shower that requires neither curtains nor doors is easily accessible and is helpful for people with allergies. Shower frames and curtains retain moisture and encourage mold growth; furthermore, plastic shower curtains may release irritants when heated.

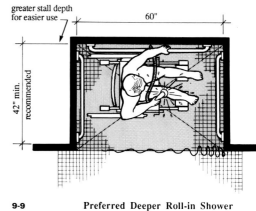

9-9   Preferred Deeper Roll-in Shower

Shower Fixtures and Controls

Ⓤ New construction should include an additional connection for the future installation of a hand-held system. Such a fixture is ideal for wheelchair use and can also be clipped to a bracket for use as a conventional shower. (Fig. 9-10) The model should require only one hand to regulate water flow and set the desired temperature. (Fig. 9-11) Install controls toward the entrance of the enclosure.

Ⓤ A lever control which prevents high temperature if the control is bumped by accident is available. This feature is also helpful to children just learning to use the controls. Another option is an integral thermometer, which allows the temperature to be preset. Both systems should include a pressure-balancing feature that prevents surges of hot and cold water. (Fig. 9-12)

Ⓤ Wall-mount a hand-held unit to allow adjustable height. The flexible hose should be at least 5 ft long,[3] but some users may require a hose as long as 7 ft. Choose a model with a water-volume control in the shower head. For clients who do not require a hand-held system, specify a multidirectional shower head that rotates 360°. (Fig. 9-13)

9-10

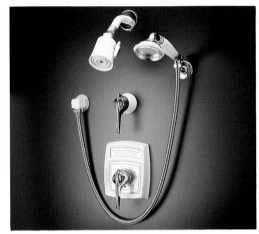

9-11

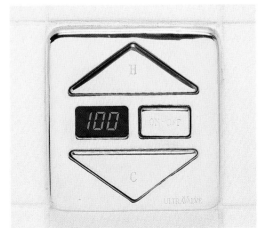

9-12

Ⓤ Specify a shower head bar for vertical adjustment that does not obstruct the grab bars. Controls must be carefully placed. (Fig. 9-14) For children, a second set of controls should be installed at a height no greater than 3 ft. As an alternative for children, a sensor could be used to automatically start the shower upon entering. The temperature can be preset to prevent a burn.

Shower Accessories

Ⓤ A shower shelf or caddie can prevent soap, shampoos, and accessories from slipping out of reach. Choose one in solid brass, plastic, or stainless steel to prevent corrosion and rust, and make sure that it drains easily. (Fig. 9-15) Recess a soap holder so that it does not interfere with wheelchair use and transfer. (Fig. 9-16) Clients may find it easier to use a liquid soap dispenser.

Ⓤ Plan multilevel soap dispensers or self-draining soap dishes. A self-draining storage space for hair care products is also helpful.

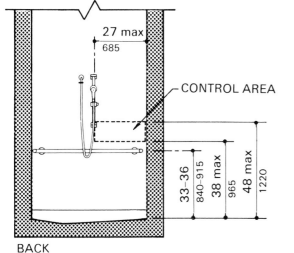

BACK
9-14

9-15

9-16

BATHTUBS

[U] A soak in the bathtub relieves pain for many people, but the design can make it difficult to get in and out. It can be especially difficult to transfer from a wheelchair into a poorly sized tub. For wheelchair access, the height of the tub should match the height of the chair seat (approximately 19 in for an average adult-sized wheelchair).[4]

[U] Lever controls are helpful to everyone and should be included whether or not the initial bathroom installation is accessible. Even the diverter should be controlled by a lever.

Bathtub Seats

[U] A seat installed on the end of bathtub is most helpful when transferring from a wheelchair. A platform on the approachable end of the tub allows the user to enter the tub. The extra length of the tub and seat may extend the space in the bathroom to allow a 5-ft turnaround space for wheelchair access. (Fig. 9-17)

[U] Bevel the edge of the seat so that it can be used as a headrest, and slant the end of the tub to make it easy to slide into the tub from the seat. For additional comfort, the slant may be contoured for extra back support. A fold-down utility tray is another convenience.

[U] For people who do not have the strength to lower themselves into the tub, install a hand-held shower to use from the seat. The controls should be lowered and installed on the long wall of the tub.

[U] If a platform cannot be added to the end of the tub, consider a movable seat that fits over the tub. The shower curtain should have a slit to fit over the seat. Bathtub transfer seats are available without backs if this support is not necessary. If a back is needed, make sure it is textured. The seat should have adjustable legs and nonskid rubber tips.

[⊪] Children can be bathed in a child seat or on a bathing table that fits in the tub. One innovative bathtub design incorporates a stationary tray and a rotating tub to ease entry and exit.

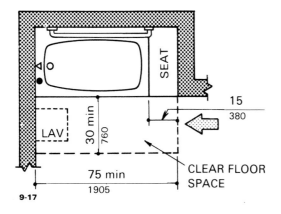

9-17

Types of Bathtubs

Ⓤ Generally, a bathtub should have a flat (not round) bottom for stability. The floor of the tub should be slip-resistant. (Fig. 9-18) If it isn't, add a nonslip bath mat that runs the full length of the tub. Look for tubs with narrow rims or handles that can be grasped when getting in and out. (Fig. 9-19)

◉ Use a contrasting stripe to identify the bathtub rim and base perimeter. Vertical stripes in the tub will help to identify the amount of water through refraction or "bending" of the stripes at the level of the water.

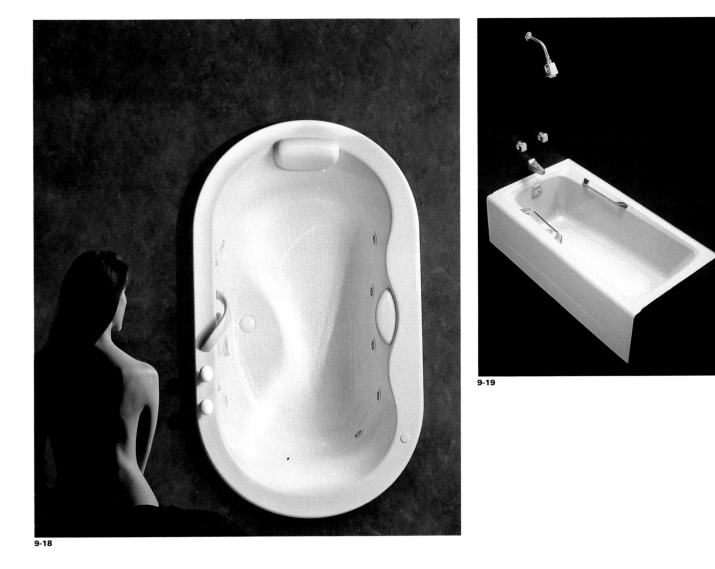

9-18

9-19

9-20

U Some doors on tubs swing up or open out for easy access. (Fig. 9-20) These doors are tightly sealed and can be used with a whirlpool bath. A hemiplegic tub with a swing-up door can be ordered for a left or right approach, allowing full use of the strong side of the body while transferring and using tub controls. A high-volume drain allows the tub to be quickly emptied before exiting.

U A spa can be made accessible to many people through the addition of a series of steps, the highest of which should be at the height of a wheelchair seat (about 19 in).[5] The user can slide from one step to the next, employing natural buoyancy to help with transfer. (Fig. 9-21)

9-21

9-22

9-23

Bathtub Controls

U Choose a lever-type faucet and drain control for easy operation. (Fig. 9-22) Controls will be more convenient if they are set toward the approach side. (Fig. 9-23) To eliminate controls, specify an automatic fill system, which programs use and presets the temperature and water level. This is especially helpful if sensitivity to temperature is a factor. (Fig. 9-24)

9-24

TOILETS AND BIDETS

Public Toilets

U UFAS and ADAAG codes covering public toilet installation do not always require sufficient wheelchair space to make a U turn in the stall or to transfer from a side approach. The National Building Code of Canada, however, requires a stall nearly 5 by 5 ft,[6] and Florida requires a minimum space of 5 ft 8 in by 5 ft 8 in.[7] Provide 42 in of adjacent space on the approach side to park the wheelchair during transfer. Each stall should have toe clearance of 9 in and door swings that meet ADAAG. Stalls should also be equipped with gravity-closing hinges.

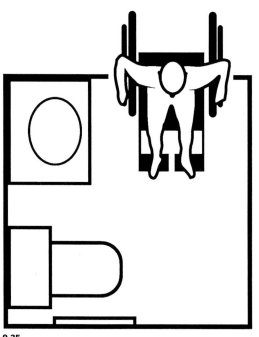

9-25

U A sink in the toilet space allows for additional privacy to clean up. (Fig. 9-25) Consider installing a unisex bathroom, which allows a spouse or aide to accompany a person who needs help. (Fig. 9-26) To save space, recess the sink in the clear space required next to the toilet. (Fig. 9-27)

U Urinals should be specified with a maximum rim height of 17 in. Children in wheelchairs require a rim height of 14 in, with flush controls no higher than 32 in.[8] A clear floor space of 30 by 48 in should be provided in front of each urinal. Privacy shields should not extend past the front edge of the urinal into the clear floor space. The urinals should be wall-mounted a minimum of 14 in from the wall.[9] Trough-type and floor wash-down urinals are not accessible. (Fig. 9-28)

9-27

9-26

9-28

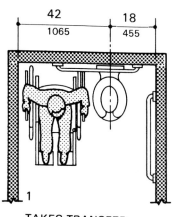

42 18
1065 455

1

TAKES TRANSFER
POSITION,
REMOVES
ARMREST, SETS
BRAKES

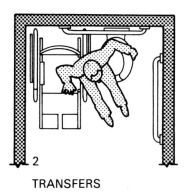

2

TRANSFERS

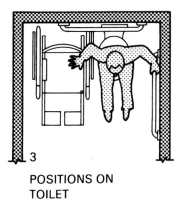

3

POSITIONS ON
TOILET

9-29

Toilets to Meet Special Needs

The design of the toilet, the height of the installation, and the approach must all be considered for wheelchair use. The toilet can be approached in several different ways. In a residence, the client may transfer into a shower wheelchair, which can roll over the toilet without an additional transfer. The client can also transfer directly from the wheelchair to the front or side of the toilet. (Fig. 9-29)

Elongated toilets are easier to use when transferring or aligning with the shower wheelchair. (Fig. 9-30) Choose a seat adjustable to wheelchair height (15 to 19 in). (Some designers prefer a height of 15 in to accommodate all users.[10]) The lower height range is also necessary to allow clearance when using a shower wheelchair. The seat height can always be raised by attaching an elevated seat if necessary.

9-30

For bowel and bladder care, specify a lower toilet with a higher seat, leaving a gap between the two. For the bowel program, for example, it may be necessary to reach into this gap. Specify a seat with an opening in the front. (Fig. 9-31) A flat or padded lid is more comfortable to lean against than one that is crowned or dished.

 Most toilets are too high to easily empty a leg bag. The lip of the toilet needs to be below the level of the drainage tube and the leg will have to be elevated to this level to empty the bag. Wall-mounted toilets can be installed at the proper height and are easier to clean since they have no base. The clearance below provides extra floor space for wheelchair footrests. (Fig. 9-32)

For ease of maintenance, the toilet can be installed in the shower and used as a shower seat. Use a padded or nonslip bench seat for transfer. A toilet in the shower will also simplify clean-up after a bowel and bladder program. (Fig. 9-33) Plan the sink and mirror outside this area to keep the mirror from fogging.

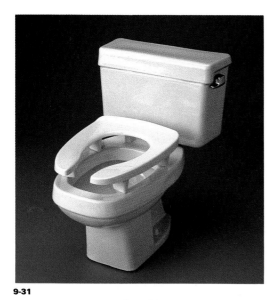

9-31

9-32

9-33

9-34

9-35

Ⓤ One toilet model uses warm water for washing and warm air for drying rather than toilet tissue. This type is especially helpful for people who find it difficult to manipulate tissue. A bidet can also be used for washing. (Fig. 9-34) A portable unit is also available. (Fig. 9-35)

A wall-mounted toilet can be installed as high as necessary for people who have trouble sitting and rising. For the bowel program a low stool may be required, elevating the feet to facilitate elimination.

Ⓤ Make sure the stop valve on the toilet is easy to use and within reach. The flushing lever should also be on the approach side,[11] and the toilet should be easy to flush. If possible, it should be neutrally handed. A toilet flush lever extension may be needed. Sensors can also be added for automatic flushing. Some flush valves in back of the toilet seat can be uncomfortable.

Ⓤ For a quieter water flow, specify pipes with as large a cross section as possible, and install low-pressure cisterns instead of high-pressure heads. People with hearing differences need quieter bathrooms to maximize their sense of hearing. People with speech differences who need to be clearly heard and people with differences in vision who depend more on their sense of hearing also appreciate reduced ambient noise.

Toilet Accessories

A transfer board may help in sliding from a wheelchair onto a toilet. Select a toilet seat with a wide bench that is easier to grasp when transferring.

If a seat with arms is needed for support, make sure the arms are adjustable to the most comfortable height. Arms that extend to the floor are more stable than arms that rest on the toilet bowl.

Ⓤ A tissue dispenser should be 19 in high so that grab bars do not interfere with its use. A toilet tissue holder with a controlled flow may be helpful. The dispenser should be mounted slightly in front of the toilet and should be recessed so it will not interfere with the wheelchair approach. (Fig. 9-36) Consider two tissue dispensers for a constant supply.

9-36

BATHROOM SINKS

U The type of sink, the location, and the accessories are all important factors in wheelchair access. Pedestal sinks can be used with wheelchair footrests spread apart, but sinks with legs limit access. (Fig. 9-37) Wall-mounted sinks are easy to wheel under if properly installed. Deeper wall-mounted sinks (over 17 in from the wall) must be supported by extra bracing. Many wheelchair lavatories are cantilevered without bracing (up to a depth of 27 in), which may cause problems if the sink is ever needed for support.

U Water supply and drain pipes can be plumbed in a horizontally offset position or located in the wall to free knee space. Eliminate sharp or abrasive edges around the perimeter of the knee space or below the sink. Insulate pipes under approachable sinks or add a removable cover to prevent burns. Plastic pipe may not require insulation if the maximum hot water temperature does not exceed 120°F.[12] Thermostatic controls limit maximum temperature and prevent sudden changes.

U The height of the sink is critical in accommodating the needs of people with different ranges of motion. To be used from a standing position, the rim of the sink should be between 32 and 36 in high, depending on user height. People in wheelchairs need a rim no higher than 34 in, and a knee space of 27 in.[13] (Fig. 9-38) Children in wheelchairs require a rim that is no higher than 30 in and a knee space of at least 24 in.[14] A clear floor space of 30 by 48 in should be provided, extending under the sink a maximum of 19 in. To meet all of these needs, specify an adjustable-height sink. (Fig. 9-39)

9-37

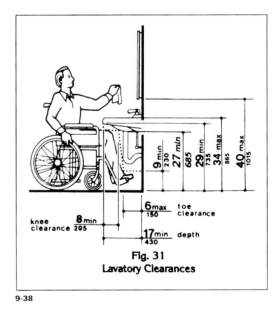

Fig. 31
Lavatory Clearances

9-38

9-39

9-40

9-41

9-42

⊙ For people with differences in vision, identify the edge of the sink area by contrasting with a color. (Fig. 9-40) Color-coded hot and cold water controls are also helpful.

FAUCETS AND CONTROLS

Ⓤ A single-lever faucet can be easily controlled with one hand; (Fig. 9-41) spring-loaded faucets take more strength to operate. Mount faucets and controls on the front apron of the counter or to the side of the sink to improve reach. For anyone who has trouble with faucet controls, a faucet is available that senses any object underneath and flows at a safe, preset temperature. (Fig. 9-42)

Ⓤ A faucet with a self-closing valve can be helpful to people with differences in coordination. It can be set to open and close the flow at preset intervals, without the use of external controls. If a self-closing valve is used, the faucet should remain open for at least 10 seconds.[15] A temperature control will prevent burns. Set the mix valve at a temperature of 115°F to start, and do not exceed 120°F.[16]

Ⓤ If the sink is used to wash hair, use a gooseneck faucet, which is easer to control than a hand-held spray. (Fig. 9-43)

Ⓤ For people with differences in hearing, the noise created by water flow should be reduced. Specify quiet ball cocks designed to give a smooth flow and aerating nozzles on taps. Reduce the water pressure as much as possible.

9-44

VANITIES

🇺 A wall-mounted sink and vanity with a knee space is useful for people in wheelchairs as well as for others who may need to sit while using the sink. (Fig. 9-44) To meet a variety of differences in use and user size, the height should be adjustable from 28 to 34 in.

🇺 For people with allergies, solid synthetic vanity tops are preferable to laminates adhered to pressboard or particleboard since both are manufactured with formaldehyde. The corners of the vanity should be rounded if they extend into the room around the sink. It's easy to bump into a corner when approaching the toilet or bending over while dressing. (Fig. 9-45)

9-45

BATHROOM STORAGE

Storage areas in the bathroom are often insufficient and require extra planning. With higher cabinets, interior shelves should be of reinforced glass or clear plastic to make the contents more visible from a seated position. Keep medications in a medicine cabinet, not on the sink. Medications can serve as a constant reminder of illness and also pose a danger to children. People with reduced manual dexterity should store medication in plastic vials rather than breakable glass bottles.

A medicine cabinet mounted to the side of the sink will be more convenient for access from a wheelchair than a cabinet mounted above the sink. (Fig. 9-46) If space is at a premium, consider mounting the cabinet on the splash between the countertop and an adjustable mirror above the sink. The cabinet should have sliding panels suspended on nylon rollers or a door with spring-loaded hinges.

Drawers beside the sink area, perhaps in a cabinet on wheels, can fill most remaining bathroom storage needs. Extra drawers can be mounted in the kick space that has been elevated for wheelchair access. These drawers may be difficult to reach, especially from a wheelchair, but they can provide needed space for seldom-used items. On all drawers, C grip handles should be horizontal and centered.

It may be more convenient to store towels in a cabinet close to the shower (and close to the washer and dryer if these are located in the bathroom). Stack extra towels on the back of the toilet if storage space is at a premium. A roll of paper towels in the bathroom is helpful for a fast cleanup.

9-46

GRAB BARS

U Grab bars, sinks, and towel bars must withstand tremendous force (250 lb/ft), including bending, shear, and tensile forces.[17] To help meet this standard, install grab bars with wood screws into studs, blocking, or plywood reinforcement. (Fig. 9-47) Molly bolts, nails, or screws into gypsum board are not adequate. With prefabricated showers, the blocking or plywood must contact the plastic over the entire reinforced area.[18]

U Grab bars should not break or chip. They should have no sharp or abrasive edges, and they must not rotate within their fittings. An oval design requires less strength to grasp than a circular bar. (Fig. 9-48)

U The color of the grab bars should contrast with the wall to ensure quick and accurate eye/hand coordination in an emergency. (Fig. 9-49) Chrome and metallic bars may produce reflected glare or blend in with the wall. Textured finishes are available for a sure grip.

U A grab bar is often used by bracing the forearm between the bar and the wall for support. Install the grab bar no more than 1 1/2 in from the wall or the entire arm could slip through the opening.[19]

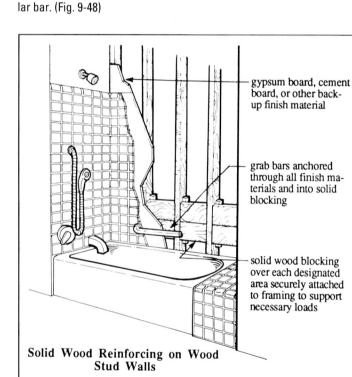

gypsum board, cement board, or other back-up finish material

grab bars anchored through all finish materials and into solid blocking

solid wood blocking over each designated area securely attached to framing to support necessary loads

Solid Wood Reinforcing on Wood Stud Walls

9-47

9-48

9-49

ADAAG requires one horizontal grab bar at the foot of the tub when a tub seat is used at the head. Two horizontal grab bars should be placed on the long wall. (Fig. 9-50) Diagonal grab bars are not suggested by ADAAG or UFAS and should not be used to replace required grab bars. The height of the grab bar will vary according to the size and ability of the client. Grab bars may have to be lowered as much as 9 in for use by children.

A transfer bar may be helpful over the bathtub; it should be installed on a ceiling trolley track or a ceiling eyebolt above the tub (with a minimum capacity of 300 lbf). The ceiling may need to be reinforced to install this bolt or track.

Grab bars may also be necessary for transferring to a shower wheelchair. If the doorway to the bathroom cannot be widened for wheelchair access, the client may have the strength to transfer to the shower wheelchair through the doorway. In this case, grab bars should be installed on both sides of the doorway for support in transferring.

In most showers, grab bars should be installed at a height of 33 to 36 in on all sides. (Fig. 9-51) When a shower seat is wall-mounted, no grab bar is needed along that wall. Shower grab bars for children should be no higher than 27 in.[20] For standing users, grab bars should be installed just below elbow height.[21] A vertical grab bar at the entrance may be desirable for a standing user if placed to meet individual needs. Vertical grab bars must not conflict with horizontal grab bars for wheelchair use. (Fig. 9-52)

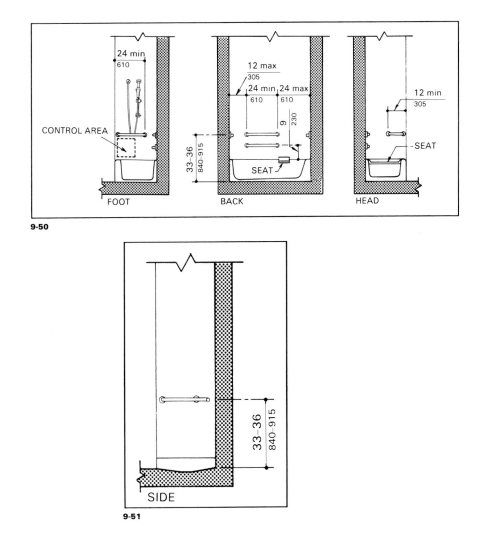

9-50

9-51

9-52

For the easiest approach to the toilet, a grab bar should be located behind the toilet and on one side. (Fig. 9-53) Install them at a height of 33 to 36 in, depending on the user. The bars should be long enough to allow an unobstructed movement.

People with strength differences prefer grab bars on both sides of the toilet, and people in wheelchairs need one side clear for the approach. A swing-up assistance bar can meet both of these needs. (Fig. 9-54)

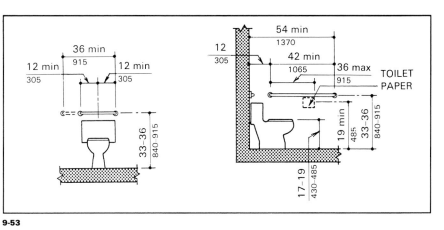

9-53

9-54

BATHROOM ACCESSORIES

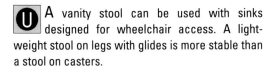 In public spaces, installed waste receptacles and recessed towel dispensers should not project into the clear space by more than 4 in. (Fig. 9-55) Coin slots and controls should be no higher than 4 ft (3 ft for children).[22] Install soap and towel dispensers on the same wall as the sinks or on the surface of the counter.

U A vanity stool can be used with sinks designed for wheelchair access. A light-weight stool on legs with glides is more stable than a stool on casters.

U Add a bench in the bathroom to help in transfer and dressing. Hooks and shelves are also helpful. (Fig. 9-56)

U The bathroom mirror must be low enough to reflect the wheelchair user's image. In most cases, it will have to be installed to the top of the splash.

U The bottom of a permanently installed mirror should be no higher than 40 in[23] (34 in for children[24]). If the mirror cannot be lowered to this height, it should be tilted with a wedge-shaped shim. A tilted mirror distorts the image but offers a fuller view than a flat mirror. Full-length mirrors 1 ft by 4 ft 8 in are appropriate for wheelchair use. They should be installed no lower than 9 in.

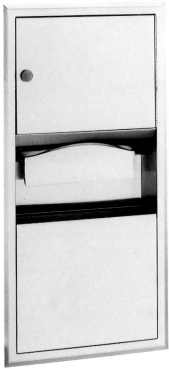

9-55

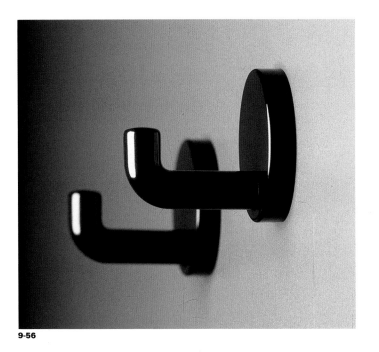

9-56

UTILITY SPACES

Save needless trips to the hamper by placing the washer and dryer in the bathroom. The bathroom sink can be used for touch-ups and the counter for clothes sorting. Install an ironing board that swivels out from under the counter, drops down from the wall, (Fig. 9-57) or pulls out of a drawer. Portable ironing boards are awkward to set up from a wheelchair and are bulky to store.

Most people cannot reach the bottom of a top-loading washer from a wheelchair. Front-loading machines also make it easier to lift wet and heavy clothes. (Fig. 9-58) Side-hinged doors allow closer wheelchair access than bottom-hinged doors.

Specify a dryer with the lint filter on the side or front, not in back. Look for models with the controls on the front. Touch controls are easier to use but are also more accessible to children.

Raised labels can be used on appliances to identify controls, marking the start of each cycle. Some manufacturers' have control covers in braille or large lettering to help with vision differences. Many washers and dryers are equipped with bells or buzzers that sound when a cycle is completed.

Consider recessing a top-loading washer in the floor to improve reach. Be sure to install a drain in the recessed area, because an overflow can harm the motor.

As an alternative, consider a front-loading washer and dryer placed one on top of the other. This setup is also helpful for users who have difficulty bending. If small items are still out of reach, suggest washing them in a zippered mesh bag that can be lifted out of the washer or dryer with tongs.

Accessories can be very helpful in handling clothes. Install a retractable clothesline or wall-mounted hanger over the bathtub within reach. Add a pull-out basket under a counter to be used as a hamper.

9-57

9-58

Appendix I Commercial Space Plan

1. For people who have trouble adjusting from light to dark areas, allow natural light into entrance areas through windows and glass doors. People with hearing differences need as much natural light as possible to distinguish facial expressions and body movements and to read lips. At least one window wall per room is recommended.

2. Consider U-shaped, V-shaped, or circular seating arrangements with swivel chairs to allow clear vision.

3. Keep the lavatory as close as possible to the toilet for easy clean-up after a bowel and bladder program.

4. Closets with a full front opening are more accessible than closets with walls returning to the doors on either side. Heavy or bulky objects should be stored below shoulder height and above hip height. For people who have trouble reaching to the floor, install a shelf at least 9 in above the floor. In a clothes closet, place another shelf directly above the clothes rod, and be sure the rod is at a reachable height (between 4 ft and 4 ft 6 in). An adjustable rod may be helpful.

5. Provide an accessible closet that is large enough to store a collapsible wheelchair. Allow sufficient space around the door (5 by 5 ft) to place two wheelchairs side by side for transfer.

6. A sideways approach to storage areas allows maximum accessibility. A clear floor space (2 ft 6 in by 4 ft) should be provided in front of all storage areas.

7. Remember that a doorway width of 3 ft is necessary for wheelchair passage. This allows the required 2 ft 8 in of clearance together with a little extra elbow room.

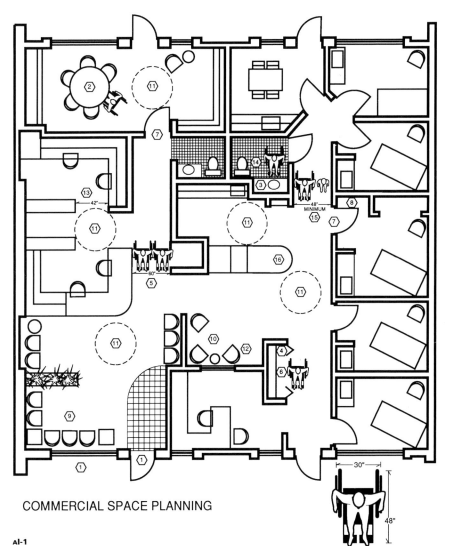

COMMERCIAL SPACE PLANNING

AI-1

177

8. Install doors 1 ft away from room corners, and hinge them on the corner side of the room. This allows additional storage space behind doors. Storage space which is reachable from a wheelchair is always at a premium.

9. Seating should not be planned facing windows since glare can be distracting. Reading chairs should be placed so that light comes over the shoulder, not on the face of the person seated.

10. Do not plan side-by-side seating, which is difficult. For people who have mobility differences do not plan side-by-side seating. Instead, plan seating positions that allow conveniently close conversations (seating no farther apart than 5 ft 6 in). For people with vision differences, even closer seating may be necessary. Avoid arrangements that face such distractions as outside doors or glaring windows.

11. Provide a clear turning radius of 60 in for wheelchair use.

12. Allow sufficient space for a wheelchair in any alcoves planned on the perimeter of the room.

13. Plan sufficient space to open drawers. This may require a wider hallway to allow clearance past an open drawer. Check the floor plan for wheelchair clearances where drawers and furniture are being used.

14. Plan companion bathrooms (unisex) and a lavatory in the toilet stall. Allow clear floor space for a forward approach to the sink.

15. A minimum hallway width of 4 ft is required to allow passage of a wheelchair user and ambulatory person. This wider width is also appropriate for those who use mobility aids.

16. Collisions often occur at hallway intersections. If these areas cannot be eliminated from the design, be sure corners are beveled, rounded, or made of glass. Corridors that intersect at right angles are easiest for people with vision problems to negotiate.

Appendix II Residential Space Plan

1. Install a bathroom window to the side of the sink to allow a wheelchair user to reach window controls and to see out the window. Remember, however, that window will take up wall space that could otherwise be used for storage.
2. Leave floor space around windows to allow operation of window hardware.
3. Windows and strong lights should not be in the direct line of sight when entering the front door.
4. Stacking closets can be used as an elevator space if the need arises at a later date.
5. To save effort, limit the number of doorways or plan to leave doorways open. Replace some doors with curtains where sound control is not a problem.
6. Doors to confined spaces (e.g., bathrooms and wheel-in closets) should swing out. In-swinging doors are more difficult to close behind wheelchairs and an ambulatory person may fall and become trapped behind an in-swinging door.
7. Remember that a doorway width of 3 ft is helpful for wheelchair passage.
8. The entryway must be at least 5 by 5 ft for wheelchair access if the door does not swing into the area. If the entry has two hinged doors in a series, make sure there is clearance of at least 4 ft between the doors.
9. Each room should include a circular clear space of 5 ft for a "U" turn in a wheelchair. This space can extend under the bathroom sink or kitchen counter, since wheelchair footrests require more turning space than armrests.
10. Accessible routes should be considered between rooms in the house and between the entryway and the garage.

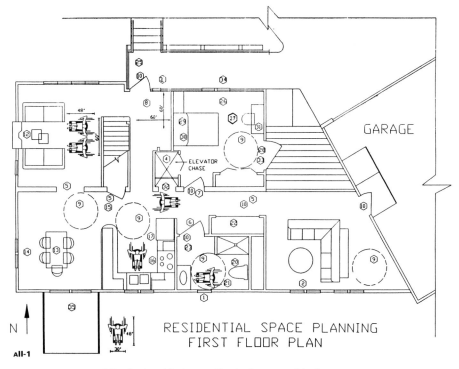

RESIDENTIAL SPACE PLANNING
FIRST FLOOR PLAN

11. A closet between the bedroom and bathroom is a nice convenience.
12. If planning a fireplace, use tempered glass doors to prevent wheelchair damage. A deep hearth (9 in) with rounded corners serves the same purpose. Allow a 4- by 5-ft clear space in the furniture floor plan to accommodate two people in wheelchairs.
13. Plan the breakfast area close to the kitchen counter to shorten the distance for serving and clearing.
14. If possible, plan a window in the dining room, particularly if the client lives alone and would enjoy an entertaining view during the meal.
15. Plan a minimum width of 42 in for the traffic lane from the kitchen to the dining table to allow space for use of a serving cart from a

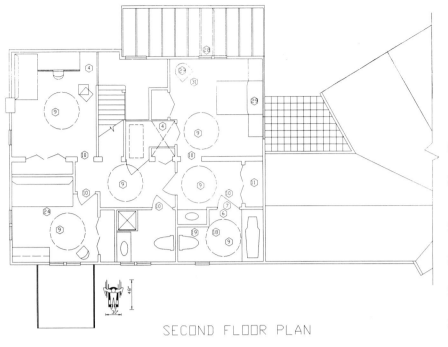

SECOND FLOOR PLAN

All-2

wheelchair. If there is no table in the kitchen, keep the dining room table close to the kitchen so that it can be used for food preparation.

16. Plan a U-shaped kitchen with open counter space next to the refrigerator and the oven. This design also allows the client to wheel under the counter and the sink. Counters should be adjustable (between 28 and 36 in) or lowered to a minimum height to maintain wheelchair clearance.

17. Allow a clear floor space of 2 ft 6 in by 4 ft before all installed appliances.

18. The bathroom should connect to the bedroom to allow privacy while dressing. Many people in wheelchairs dress on the bed after using the bathroom.

19. Consider the preferred transfer technique in planning the space in the bathroom. It can be arranged to allow either a left-handed or right-handed approach.

20. The shower may need to be placed close to the toilet for clean-up after changing a leg bag or other aspects of a bowel program.

21. Allow clear space for a forward approach to the sink.

22. If noise control is not a problem, consider installing the washer and dryer in the hallway between the bathroom and bedroom. This design is convenient and saves time and effort.

23. Isolate or soundproof noisy rooms. Locate a utility room or workshop away from such areas as the living room, bedroom, and den. Sound transmitted through the walls may make it difficult to hear in other rooms. Position the bathroom to achieve olfactory and acoustic isolation.

24. Privacy can be improved by planning children's bedrooms away from the master bedroom.

25. Make sure the entryway is designed to provide visual privacy to the rest of the house when the front door is open.

26. Include guest facilities if possible and attendant care facilities if necessary.

27. There should be clearance of 3 ft at the foot and at least one side of the bed.

28. Plan an accessible emergency exit from the bedroom.

29. Because glare can be distracting, the bedroom should be planned so that the bed does not face a window. Reading chairs should be placed so that light comes over the shoulder, not on the face, of the person seated.

30. To prevent exposure to drafts, never place the head of a bed against or under a window. Make sure walls are well insulated if the bed is to be placed against the outside wall. If the client spends more time in the bedroom than in other living spaces, enlarge the bedroom and include extra storage to prevent needless trips.

31. Provide a comfortable seat near the bed for visitors. Consider an arrangement that allows work to be done in the bedroom.

32. Provide a centrally located closet for storing maintenance equipment. A sideways approach will allow maximum accessibility. A clear floor space (2 ft 6 in by 4 ft) should be provided in front of all storage areas.

33. Specify a wide door (39 in) to accommodate large pieces of furniture. For people who spend daytime in bed, they may wish to move the bed outdoors for a change of pace. This door can also be an outside emergency exit.

34. Plan windows to allow easier escape routes. The sill width, window position, frame design, and outside landing must all be considered. Vision may be limited from windows higher than 3 ft. A shallow exterior windowsill allows a clear view.

35. A client with limited circulation may prefer warmer rooms. Choose a house plan with southern exposures in the areas where the client spends the most time.

References

Preface

1. Roy Alexander, ed., "Schools of Tomorrow," *Time* 76 (September 1960): 74–79.
2. Gerry M. O'Connor, "Design: Remodeling for the Handicapped and Elderly," *Remodeling Contractor* (November 1986): 48.
3. National Center for Health Statistics, 1988.
4. O'Connor, "Design," 47.
5. Americans With Disabilities Act Accessibility Guidelines, 1991.
6. Ulrich, Roger S., "Effects of Interior Design on Wellness: Theory and Recent Scientific Research" (Paper delivered at the Third Symposium of Healthcare Interior Design, San Francisco, 15–18 November 1990): 13.
7. O'Connor, "Design," 47.
8. O'Connor, "Design," 48.
9. Walter B. Kleeman, *The Challenge of Interior Design.* (Boston: CBI Publishing, 1981), 149.
10. Lenny M. Rickman and Carol E. Soble, *Home for a Lifetime: A New Market Niche for NAHB Builders/Remodelers.* (Washington, DC: National Association of Home Builders National Research Center, 1988), 11.
11. Life Care Centers, *Our Commitment to Serving the Elderly.* (Cleveland, Tennessee: Author, 1988), 4.
12. Rickman, "Home," 3.
13. Markle Foundation, *Pioneers on the Frontier of Life: Aging in America* (New York: Markle Foundation, 1988), 1.
14. Internal Revenue Service, Department of the Treasury. 1990. *Medical and Dental Expenses* Publication #502. Washington DC: Government Printing Office, 1.
15. Bartholomew, Douglas. 1991. Opening Your Door to the Disabled. *Your Company* Spring 1991: 46.
16. Kim Beasley, "Design Lines: The Cost of Accessibility," *Paraplegia News* (June 1990): 42.
17. Beasley, "Design Lines," 42.

Chapter 1

1. *Uniform Federal Accessibility Standards,* 24 CFR subtitle A 4-1-90 (Washington, D.C.: Government Printing Office, 1990).
2. Americans With Disabilities Act Accessibility Guidelines, 1991.
3. UFAS, 1990.
4. ADAAG, 1991.
5. Ibid.
6. Ibid.
7. Robert Sorensen. *Design for Accessibility.* (New York: McGraw-Hill, 1979), 158.

8. American National Standards Institute, *American National Standard for Buildings and Facilities Providing Accessibility and Usability for Physically Handicapped People,* ANSI A117.1-1986 (New York: ANSI, 1986).
9. ADAAG, 1991.
10. Ibid.
11. North Carolina State Building Code Council, *North Carolina State Building Code,* vol. 1-C (Raleigh: NCSBCC, 1989).
12. UFAS, 1990.
13. NCSBCC, 1989.
14. Ibid.
15. ADAAG, 1991.
16. Ibid.
17. Ibid.
18. Ibid.
19. NCSBCC, 1989.
20. ADAAG, 1991.
21. Ibid.

Chapter 2

1. North Carolina State Building Code Council, *North Carolina State Building Code,* vol. 1-C (Raleigh: NCSBCC, 1989).
2. Americans With Disabilities Act Accessibility Guidelines, 1991.
3. Janet Reizenstein Carpman, Myron A. Grant and Deborah A. Simmons. *Design That Cares.* (Chicago: American Hospital Publishing, Inc., 1986), 228.
4. Lorraine G. Hiatt, "Long-Term-Care Facilities," *Journal of Health Care Interior Design* 2 (1990): 200.
5. Robert J. Kobet, "Allergies in Architecture" (Paper delivered at the regional conference of the American Association of Otolaryngologic Allergists, San Antonio, Tex., 18 May 1987).
6. Hiatt, "Long-Term-Care," 199.
7. Walter B. Kleeman, *The Challenge of Interior Design.* (Boston: CBI Publishing, 1981), 79.
8. Hiatt, "Long-Term-Care," 200.
9. Carpman, *Design That Cares,* 228.
10. Kleeman, "Challenge," 76.
11. Robert J. Kobet, "The Tight House Syndrome: Causes and Cures" (Paper delivered at the American Society of Interior Designers National Conference, Washington, D.C., August 1988).
12. Kobet, "Allergies."
13. ADAAG, 1991.
14. Kobet, "Allergies."
15. Carol Venolia, "Healing Environments," *Journal of Health Care Interior Design* 2 (1990): 133.

16. Carpman, *Design That Cares,* 240.
17. Hiatt, "Long-Term-Care," 201.
18. Kobet, "The Tight House Syndrome."
19. Robert Marshall, "Carpet as an Acoustical Material," *Canadian Interiors* 1 (1970): 36–39.
20. G. W. Evans and S. Cohen, "Environmental Stress," in *Handbook of Environmental Psychology,* ed. D. Stokols and I. Altman (New York: John Wiley, 1987), 571–610.
21. Carpman, *Design That Cares,* 228.
22. ADAAG, 1991.

Chapter 3

1. Walter B. Kleeman, *The Challenge of Interior Design* (Boston: CBI Publishing, 1981), 61.
2. Leon A. Pastalan, *Aging and Human Visual Function* (New York: Alan R. Liss, 1982), 324.
3. Lorraine G. Hiatt, "The Color and Use of Color in Environments for Older People" *Nursing Homes* 1981, 30(3): 18–22.
4. Pastalan, *Aging,* 325.
5. Lorraine G. Hiatt, Long-Term-Care Facilities. *Journal of Health Care Interior Design* 2 (1990): 200.
6. JoAnn L. Shroyer and J. Thomas Hutton, "Alzheimer's Disease: Strategies for Designing Interiors" *American Society of Interior Designers Report* 1989, 15(2): 10–11.
7. Judith K. Mousseau, "Design Specialty: A Case for Color" *American Society of Interior Designers Report* 1987, 13(2): 16.
8. Kleeman, "Challenge," 152.
9. Shroyer and Hutton, "Alzheimer's Disease," 12.
10. Gary Coates and Susanne Siepl-Coates, "Vidarkliniken: A Study of the Anthroposophical Healing Center in Jarna, Sweden" (Paper delivered at the Built Form and Culture Research Conference, Arizona State University, Tempe, November 1989).
11. Hiatt, "The Color and Use of Color," 21.
12. Pastalan, *Aging,* 324.
13. Robert J. Kobet, "The Tight House Syndrome: Causes and Cures" (Paper delivered at the American Society of Interior Designers National Conference, Washington, D.C., August 1988).
14. Coates and Siepl-Coates, "Vidarkliniken."
15. Milner, Margaret, *Breaking Through the Deafness Barrier: Environmental Accommodations for Hearing Impaired People.* (Washington, DC: Physical Plant Department, Gallaudet College, 1979) 9.
16. Robert Sorensen, *Design for Accessibility* (New York: McGraw-Hill, 1979), 214.
17. J. R. Carpman, M. A. Grant, and D. A. Simmons, *Design That Cares* (Chicago: American Hospital Publishing, 1986), 223.
18. Virginia Beamer Weinhold, *Interior Finish Materials for Health Care Facilities* (Springfield, Ill.: Charles C. Thomas, 1988), 125.
19. Ibid., 127.
20. Ibid., 135.

Chapter 4

1. Walter B. Kleeman, *The Challenge of Interior Design.* (Boston: CBI Publishing, 1981), 192.
2. Americans With Disabilities Act Accessibility Guidelines, 1991.

3. Robert J. Kobet. "The Tight House Syndrome: Causes and Cures" (Paper delivered at the American Society of Interior Designers National Conference, Washington, D.C., August 1988).
4. ADAAG, 1991.
5. ADAAG, 1991.
6. North Carolina State Building Code Council, *North Carolina State Building Code* vol. 1-C Raleigh: NCSBCC, 1989).
7. American National Standards Institute, *American National Standard for Buildings and Facilities Providing Accessibility and Usability for Physically Handicapped People,* ANSI A117.1-1986 (New York: ANSI, 1986).
8. ADAAG, 1991.
9. NCSBCC, 1989.
10. ADAAG, 1991.
11. NCSBCC, 1989.

Chapter 5

1. Walter B. Kleeman, *The Challenge of Interior Design* (Boston: CBI Publishing, 1981), 243.
2. Virginia Beamer Weinhold, *Interior Finish Materials for Health Care Facilities* (Springfield, Ill.: Charles C. Thomas, 1988), 25.
3. Julia S. Garner and Martin S. Favero, "CDC Guidelines for Handwashing and Hospital Environmental Control, 1986," *Infection Control* 7(4): 231–243.
4. Weinhold, *Interior Finish Materials,* 24.
5. Garner and Favero, "CDC Guidelines," 233.
6. Lorraine G. Hiatt, Long-Term-Care Facilities, *Journal of Health Care Interior Design* 2 (1990): 203.
7. Robert J. Kobet, "The Tight House Syndrome: Causes and Cures" (Paper delivered at the American Society of Interior Designers National Conference, Washington, D.C., August 1988).
8. Roger Yee, "Almost Indestructible Floors with Goose Bumps" *Contract Design* (February 1991): 66.
9. Americans With Disabilities Act Accessibility Guidelines, 1991.
10. Weinhold, *Interior Finish Materials,* 85.

Chapter 6

1. Lorraine G. Hiatt, "Long-Term-Care Facilities" *Journal of Health Care Interior Design* 2 (1990): 199.
2. Walter B. Kleeman, *The Challenge of Interior Design* (Boston: CBI Publishing, 1981), 118.
3. North Carolina State Building Code Council, *North Carolina State Building Code,* vol. 1-C (Raleigh: NCSBCC, 1989).
4. Ibid., 7.2.(d).
5. Bettyann Boetticher Raschko, *Housing Interiors for the Disabled and Elderly* (New York: Van Nostrand Reinhold, 1982), 105.
6. Americans With Disabilities Act Accessibility Guidelines, 1991.
7. Kleeman, "Challenge," 121.
8. Ibid., 99.
9. M. C. Eastman and E. Kamon, "Posture and Subjective Evaluation at Flat and Slanted Desks" *Human Factors,* 1976, 18(1): 15–26.
10. NCSBCC, 1989.
11. Kleeman, "Challenge," 94.
12. Ibid., 109.
13. Ibid., 93.
14. Ibid., 265.
15. Ibid., 101.

16. Ibid., 106.
17. Hiatt, "Long-Term-Care," 205.
18. Robert J. Kobet, "Allergies in Architecture" (Paper delivered at the regional conference of the American Association of Otolaryngologic Allergists, San Antonio, Texas, 18 May 1987).
19. California Department of Consumer Affairs, *Flammability Test Procedure for Seating Furniture for Use in Public Occupancies,* tech. bulletin no. 133 (North Highlands, Calif.: CDCC, 1988).
20. Kleeman, "Challenge," 265.

Chapter 7

1. IBM National Support Center for Persons with Disabilities, *Technology for Persons with Disabilities: An Introduction* (Atlanta: IBM, 1991), 1–8.
2. Ibid., 1–8.
3. Ibid., 1–8.
4. Ibid., 1–8.
5. Ibid., 1–8.
6. Americans With Disabilities Act Accessibility Guidelines, 1991.
7. North Carolina State Building Code Council, *North Carolina State Building Code,* vol. 1-C (Raleigh: NCSBCC, 1989).
8. ADAAG, 1991.
9. Ibid.
10. Roger S. Ulrich, "Effects of Interior Design on Wellness: Theory and Recent Scientific Research" (Paper delivered at the Third Symposium of Healthcare Interior Design, San Francisco, 15–18 November 1990).
11. Janet Reizenstein Carpman, Myron A. Grant and Deborah A. Simmons. *Design That Cares.* (Chicago: American Hospital Publishing, Inc., 1986), 26.
12. Ibid., 27.
13. Ibid., 28.
14. Ibid., 28.
15. Ibid., 28.
16. ADAAG, 1991.
17. NCSBCC, 1989.
18. ADAAG, 1991.
19. ADAAG, 1991.
20. Carpman, *Design That Cares,* 52.
21. ADAAG, 1991.
22. NCSBCC, 1989.
23. Ibid., app. 1989.
24. Robert J. Kobet, "The Tight House Syndrome: Causes and Cures" (Paper delivered at the American Society of Interior Designers National Conference, Washington, D.C., August 1988).

Chapter 8

1. North Carolina State Building Code Council, *North Carolina State Building Code,* vol. 1-C (Raleigh: NCSBCC, 1989).
2. Robert J. Kobet, "The Tight House Syndrome: Causes and Cures" (Paper delivered at the American Society of Interior Designers National Conference, Washington, D.C., August 1988).
3. Walter B. Kleeman, *The Challenge of Interior Design* (Boston: CBI Publishing, 1981), 42.

4. Kenneth R. Tremblay, "Housing and Design Considerations for the Deaf," *Dimensions* (Fall/Winter 1989): 7.
5. American National Standards Institute, *American National Standard for Buildings and Facilities Providing Accessibility and Usability for Physically Handicapped People,* ANSI A117.1-1986 (New York: ANSI, 1986).
6. Americans With Disabilities Act Accessibility Guidelines, 1991.
7. Barrier Free Environments, *Adaptable Housing: The Technical Manual for Implementing Adaptable Housing Unit Specifications,* 023-000-00760-6 (Washington, D.C.: U.S. Government Printing Office, 1989), fig. 22.
8. NCSBCC, 1989.
9. ADAAG, 1991.
10. Anne Patterson, ed., "Beautiful Designs for the Handicapped," *Kitchen and Bath Concepts* (January 1987): 36.
11. ADAAG, 1991.
12. Health and Welfare, Canada, *Plumbing Fixtures,* H74-18/11-1985E (Ottawa: Ministry of Supply and Services, Canada, 1985).
13. ANSI, 4.32.5.7.

Chapter 9

1. Americans With Disabilities Act Accessibility Guidelines, 1991.
2. ADAAG, 1991.
3. ADAAG, 1991.
4. ADAAG, 1991.
5. Ibid.
6. Associate Committee on the National Building Code National Research Council of Canada, *National Building Code of Canada 1990* (Ottawa: Ministry of Supply and Services Canada, 1990).
7. Department of Community Affairs, Florida Board of Building Codes and Standards, *Accessibility Requirements Manual* (Tallahassee: FBBC&S, 1990).
8. North Carolina State Building Code Council, *North Carolina State Building Code,* vol. 1-C (Raleigh: NCSBCC, 1989).
9. Ibid., 1989.
10. Carol E. Klein, "Kitchen and Bath Design for Elderly Housing," *Commercial Renovation* (February 1988): 46.
11. ADAAG, 1991.
12. NCSBCC, 1989.
13. ADAAG, 1991.
14. NCSBCC, 1989.
15. ADAAG, 1991.
16. NCSBCC, 1989.
17. ADAAG, 1991.
18. Barrier Free Environments, *Adaptable Housing: The Technical Manual for Implementing Adaptable Housing Unit Specifications,* 023-000-00760-6 (Washington, D.C.: U.S. Government Printing Office, 1989), 46.
19. ADAAG, 1991.
20. NCSBCC, 1989.
21. Health and Welfare, Canada, *Showers* H74-18/7-1985E (Ottawa: Ministry of Supply and Services, Canada, 1985).
22. NCSBCC, 1989.
23. ADAAG, 1991.
24. NCSBCC 1989.

Illustration Credits

Chapter 1

1-1. Courtesy of Pat M. Bridges & Assoc. Builders.   **1-2.** Reprinted by permission from the Veterans Administration, VA pamphlet 26-13, April 1978.   **1-3.** Reproduced with permission from American National Standard for Buildings and Facilities Providing Accessibility and Usability for Physically Handicapped People A117.1-1986, copyright 1986 by the American National Standards Institute.   **1-4.** Reproduced with permission from American National Standard for Buildings and Facilities Providing Accessibility and Usability for Physically Handicapped People A117.1-1986, copyright 1986 by the American National Standards Institute.   **1-5.** Courtesy of Spanjier Brothers, Inc.   **1-6.** Reprinted by permission from Kim A. Beasley AIA, Design for Hospitality—Planning for Accessible Hotels and Motels. New York: Nichols Publishing, 1988, page 29.   **1-7.** Courtesy of Industrial Fabrics Association.   **1-8.** Photo courtesy of: Pella/Rolscreen Company.   **1-9.** Courtesy of Carolyn Latteier.   **1-10.** Courtesy of Garcia Imports.   **1-11.** Courtesy of American Lantern Company.   **1-12.** Reproduced by permission from the 1984 Uniform Federal Accessibility Standards by the Publications Division, U.S. General Services Administration.   **1-13.** Reproduced with permission from American National Standard for Buildings and Facilities Providing Accessibility and Usability for Physically Handicapped People A117.1-1986, copyright 1986 by the American National Standards Institute.   **1-14.** Reproduced with permission from American National Standard for Buildings and Facilities Providing Accessibility and Usability for Physically Handicapped People A117.1-1986, copyright 1986 by the American National Standards Institute.   **1-15.** Reproduced with permission from American National Standard for Buildings and Facilities Providing Accessibility and Usability for Physically Handicapped People A117.1-1986, copyright 1986 by the American National Standards Institute.   **1-16.** Courtesy of Barrier Free Environments.   **1-17.** Reproduced by permission from the 1984 Uniform Federal Accessibility Standards by the Publications Division, U.S. General Services Administration.   **1-18.** Reproduced with permission from American National Standard for Buildings and Facilities Providing Accessibility and Usability for Physically Handicapped People A117.1-1986, copyright 1986 by the American National Standards Institute.   **1-19.** Reprinted by permission from Accent Special Publications, Ideas for Making Your Home Accessible. Bloomington, Ill.: Cheever Publishing, 1986.   **1-20.** Reproduced with permission from American National Standard for Buildings and Facilities Providing Accessibility and Usability for Physically Handicapped People A117.1-1986, copyright 1986 by the American National Standards Institute.   **1-21.** Courtesy of Sunrise Medical Guardian—Guardian Products, Inc.   **1-22.** Courtesy of Loren Greenhill. Photography: Sally Reynolds.   **1-23.** Courtesy of American Olean Tile Company.   **1-24.** Courtesy of American Stair-Glide Corp.   **1-25.** Courtesy of Cheney.   **1-26.** Reproduced with permission from American National Standard for Buildings and Facilities Providing Accessibility and Usability for Physically Handicapped People A117.1-1986, copyright 1986 by the American National Standards Institute.   **1-27.** Reproduced by permission from the 1984 Uniform Federal Accessibility Standards by the Publications Division, U.S. General Services Administration.   **1-28.** Reproduced by permission from the 1984 Uniform Federal Accessibility Standards by the Publications Division, U.S. General Services Administration.   **1-29.** Reproduced by permission from the 1984 Uniform Federal Accessibility Standards by the Publications Division, U.S. General Services Administration.   **1-30.** Courtesy of Jack Bowersox AIA.   **1-31.** Reprinted by permission from Kim A. Beasley AIA, Design for Hospitality—Planning for Accessible Hotels and Motels. New York: Nichols Publishing, 1988, page 46.   **1-32.** Reproduced with permission from American National Standard for Buildings and Facilities Providing Accessibility and Usability for Physically Handicapped People A117.1-1986, copyright 1986 by the American National Standards Institute.   **1-33.** Reproduced by permission from the Americans With Disabilities Accessibility Guidelines, copyright 1991.   **1-34.** Courtesy of York Spiral Stairs.   **1-35.** Courtesy of HEWI.

Chapter 2

2-1. Courtesy of Lutron Electronics Company, Inc.   **2-2.** Courtesy of Honeywell.   **2-3.** Courtesy of Jenn-Air Company.   **2-4.** Courtesy of Lutron Electronics Company, Inc.   **2-5.** Courtesy of The Ironmonger, Inc.   **2-6.** Courtesy of Tempo Industries.   **2-7.** Courtesy of ATLANTA THERMOPLASTIC PRODUCTS, a division of NAACE INDUSTRIES, INC.   **2-8.** Courtesy of Leviton Manufacturing Co.   **2-9.** Courtesy of Cynthia Leibrock MA, ASID, Easy Access, Barrier Free Design Consultants. Illustration: Susan Behar ASID, Universal Design.   **2-10.** Reprinted by permission from Bettyann Boetticher Raschko, Housing Interiors for the Disabled and Elderly. New York: Van Nostrand Reinhold, copyright, 1982.   **2-11.** Courtesy of All-Steel Phone/Data Integration Modules.   **2-12.** Courtesy of Artemide Company.   **2-13.** Courtesy of NuTone Company.   **2-14.** Courtesy of National Products Inc.   **2-15.** Courtesy of Michael Callori, The Gilchrist Partnership. Photography: Otto Baitz.   **2-16.** Courtesy of Duro-Test Corp.   **2-17.** Reprinted by permission from Van Nostrand Reinhold, The Challenge of Interior Design. Boston: CBI Publishing Company, Inc., 1981.   **2-18.** Compliment of Halo Lighting.   **2-19.** Courtesy of Lightworks.   **2-20.** Courtesy of Tempo Industries.   **2-21.** Courtesy of Milcor/Lima Register.   **2-22.** Reproduced by permission from the Americans With Disabilities Accessibility Guidelines, copyright 1991.   **2-23.** Courtesy of Research Products Corp.   **2-24.** Courtesy of NuTone Company.   **2-25.** Courtesy of Honeywell Corporation.   **2-26.** Courtesy of Jean Roy.   **2-27.** C. Harris, *Dictionary of Architecture and Construction,* copyright 1975, McGraw-Hill. Reproduced with permission of McGraw-Hill, Inc.   **2-28.** Reproduced by permission of J.C. Penney Company Inc. 1991.   **2-29.** Courtesy of Dimango Products.   **2-30.** Courtesy of Mastervoice.   **2-31.** Courtesy of Aiphone Corporation.   **2-32.** Courtesy of NuTone Company.   **2-33.** Courtesy of Maxi-Aids.   **2-34.** Courtesy of Cynthia Leibrock MA, ASID, Easy Access, Barrier Free Design Consultants. Illustration: Susan Behar ASID, Universal Design.   **2-35.** Courtesy of Rain Bird Sales Inc.   **2-36.** Courtesy of Unity Systems Inc.   **2-37.** Courtesy of Sonic Alert Systems.   **2-38.** Reprinted by permission from Bettyann Boetticher Raschko, Housing Interiors for the Disabled and Elderly. New York: Van Nostrand Reinhold, copyright 1982.

Chapter 3

3-1. Courtesy of SpacePlanning and Interior Design, Jain Malkin Inc. Photography: John Christian.   **3-2.** Photo courtesy of: Pella/Rolscreen Company.   **3-3.** Courtesy of Benjamin Moore and Company.   **3-4.** Courtesy of Kimball Hospitality Furniture, Inc.   **3-5.** Courtesy of Innovations-in Wallcoverings.   **3-6.** Courtesy of USG Interiors.   **3-7.** Courtesy of The Harbinger Company, Inc., Calhoun, Ga.   **3-8.** Courtesy of Construction Specialties, Inc., Box 380, Muncy, Pa. 17756. Photography: Andrew D. Lautman.   **3-9.** Courtesy of Barbara Matthes.   **3-10.** Courtesy of Construction Specialties, Inc., Box 380, Muncy, Pa. 17756.   **3-11.** Courtesy of Eurotex Inc.   **3-12.** Courtesy of Cynthia Leibrock MA, ASID, Easy Access, Barrier Free Design Consultants.   **3-13.** Courtesy of Banner Scapes.   **3-14.** Courtesy of Barrisol Stretched Ceiling System, Barrisol North America, Inc.   **3-15.** Architect: Schamu, Machowski, Doo & Associates. Photographer: Frik Kvalsvik. Millwork: Walker/Welsh Associates Inc.   **3-16.** C. Harris, *Dictionary Of Architecture and Construction,* copyright 1975, McGraw-Hill. Reproduced with permission of McGraw-Hill, Inc.   **3-17.** Courtesy of Winona Manufacturing, Inc.   **3-18.** From *Interior Finish Materials for Health Care Facilities,* 1988. Springfield, Illinois. Courtesy of Charles C Thomas, Publisher.

Chapter 4

4-1. Courtesy of Andersen Corporation, Inc.   **4-2.** Courtesy of Spectus Systems   **4-3.** Courtesy of Pinecrest.   **4-4.** Courtesy of Andersen Corporation, Inc.   **4-5.** Courtesy of Joanna Western Mills.   **4-6.** Courtesy of Conrad Imports Inc.   **4-7.** Reprinted by permission from Leona K. Hawks, Housing and Home Equipment Specialist, Utah State University.   **4-8.** Courtesy of Silent Gliss USA Inc.   **4-9.** Courtesy of Industrial Fabrics Industries.   **4-10.** Reprinted by permission from Leona K. Hawks, Housing and Home Equipment Specialist, Utah State University.   **4-11.** Reprinted by permission from Leona K. Hawks, Housing and Home Equipment Specialist, Utah State University.   **4-12.** Photo courtesy of LouverDrape.®   **4-13.** Courtesy of Baker Drapery Corp.   **4-14.** Courtesy of Susan Beher ASID, Universal Design.   **4-15.** Courtesy of Andersen Corporation, Inc.   **4-16.** Courtesy of Andersen Corporation, Inc.   **4-17.** Courtesy of Ben Grafton Ltd.   **4-18.** Duro-Med Industries Inc.

4–19. Courtesy of Constantine. 4–20. Intradesign, Inc. for Le Meridien Coronado. Cynthia Forchielli, project designer. Photography: Mary E. Nichols. 4–21. Reprinted by permission from Bettyann Boetticher Raschko, Housing Interiors for the Disabled and Elderly. New York: Van Nostrand Reinhold, copyright 1982. 4–22. Courtesy of Pinecrest. 4–23. Courtesy of Stanley Magic-Door. 4–24. Courtesy of Barrier Free Environments, photography: Ron Mace. 4–25. Courtesy of Stanley Magic-Door. 4–26. Courtesy of Construction Specialties Inc. 4–27. Courtesy of Pinecrest. 4–28. Courtesy of The Ironmonger. 4–29.Courtesy of HEWI. 4–30. Courtesy of HEWI. 4–31. Courtesy of Preso-matic.

Chapter 5

5–1. From *Interior Finish Materials for Health Care Facilities,* 1988. Courtesy of Charles C Thomas, Publisher, Springfield, Illinois. 5–2. Photo by Ron Starr. 5–3. From *Interior Finish Materials for Health Care Facilities,* 1988. Courtesy of Charles C Thomas, Publisher, Springfield, Illinois. 5–4. Reproduced by permission from the 1984 Uniform Federal Accessibility Standards by the Publications Division, U.S. General Services Administration. 5–5. Courtesy of Shaw Industries Inc. 5–6. From *Interior Finish Materials for Health Care Facilities,* 1988. Courtesy of Charles C Thomas, Publisher, Springfield, Illinois. 5–7. Courtesy of Bonar and Flotex Inc. 5–8. Interior design: Jain Malkin Inc. Photographer: John Christian. 5–9. Interior Design: Jain Malkin Inc. Photographer: Michael Denny. 5–10. Reproduced with permission from American National Standard for Buildings and Facilities Providing Accessibility and Usability for Physically Handicapped People A117.1-1986, copyright 1986 by the American National Standards Institute. 5–11. Courtesy of Mercer Products Inc. 5–12. Illustration courtesy of Collins and Aikman Corporation, Floor Coverings Division, Dalton, Ga. 5–13. Interior design: Antonio F. Torrice ASID, Living and Learning Environments. Photography: Mike Spinelli Photography. 5–14. The Timeless Series acrylic/wood plank by PermaGrain Products, Inc., installed at The Boston Store, Brookfield, Wis. 5–15. From *Interior Finish Materials for Health Care Facilities,* 1988. Courtesy of Charles C Thomas, Publisher, Springfield, Illinois. 5–16. From *Interior Finish Materials for Health Care Facilities,* 1988. Courtesy of Charles C Thomas, Publisher, Springfield, Illinois. 5–17. Courtesy of Roppe. 5–18. Courtesy of Kohler Co. 5–19. Courtesy of American Olean Tile Company. Project: Pennsylvania West Chapter ASID. Interior design: Nancy Hoff Barsotti ASID. 5–20. Architecture: Brown Gimber Rodriquez Park. Interior Design: Jain Malkin Inc. Photographer: Sandra Williams. 5–21. Courtesy of American Olean Tile Company.

Chapter 6

6–1. Courtesy of Susan Behar ASID, Universal Design. Photography: Vernon Photography. 6–2. Courtesy of Custom Lamination Inc. 6–3. Courtesy of Susan Behar ASID, Universal Design. Photography: Vernon Photography. 6–4. Courtesy of Nova Technologies, Inc. 6–5. Courtesy of Joerns Healthcare Inc. 6–6. Courtesy of Wesley Allen, Inc. 6–7. Courtesy of Wesley Allen, Inc. 6–8. Courtesy of Lumex, a division of Lumex, Inc. 6–9. Courtesy of Susan Behar ASID, Universal Design. Photography: Vernon Photography. 6–10. Courtesy of Clairson International. 6–11. Courtesy of Ligne Roset USA. 6–12. Courtesy of Workstations, Inc. 6–13. Courtesy of Ello Furniture Manufacturing Co. 6–14. Courtesy of David Hawk. Architecture: Haller and Larson. 6–15. Courtesy of Susan Behar ASID, Universal Design. Photography: Vernon Photography. 6–16. Courtesy of Garcia Imports. 6–17. Courtesy of Ligne Roset USA 6–18. Reproduced with permission from American National Standard for Buildings and Facilities Providing Accessibility and Usability for Physically Handicapped People A117.1-1986, copyright 1986 by the American National Standards Institute. 6–19. Courtesy of Susan Behar ASID, Universal Design. Photography: Vernon Photography. 6–20. Reproduced with permission from American National Standard for Buildings and Facilities Providing Accessibility and Usability for Physically Handicapped People A117.1-1986, copyright 1986 by the American National Standards Institute. 6–21. Courtesy of Sico Inc. 6–22. Courtesy of Lumex, a division of Lumex, Inc. 6–23. Courtesy of Ello Furniture Manufacturing Company. 6–24. Courtesy of Kimball Healthcare Co. 6–25. Reprinted by permission from Bettyann Boetticher Raschko, Housing Interiors for the Disabled and Elderly. New York: Van Nostrand Reinhold, copyright 1982. 6–26. Susan Kallewaard Photography for Furniture. Samson-McCann. 6–27. Courtesy of Metropolitan Furniture Corp. Designer: Brian Kane. 6–28. Courtesy of Ligne Roset USA. 6–29. Courtesy of Ligne Roset USA. 6–30. Courtesy of CyMann Designs, Ltd. 6–31. Courtesy of The Knoll Group, Breuer Lac-

cio Table. 6–32. Courtesy of Workstations, Inc. 6–33. Courtesy of Cy Mann Designs, Ltd. 6–34. Courtesy of McGuire and Company. 6–35. Courtesy of McGuire and Company. 6–36. Courtesy of Howe Furniture Corporation. 6–37. Courtey of Vecta Contract. 6–38. Courtesy of The Pace Collection, Inc. 6–39. Courtesy of Palazzetti, Inc. 6–40. Courtesy of Haworth, Inc. 6–41. Courtesy of Workstations, Inc. 6–42. Courtesy of Workstations, Inc. 6–43. Courtesy of Able Office. 6–44. Courtesy of Haworth, Inc. 6–45. Courtesy of Human Factors Technology, Inc. 6–46. Courtesy of Susan Behar ASID, Universal Design. Photography: George Cott. 6–47. Courtesy of Add Interior Systems, Inc. 6–48. Courtesy of Add Interior Systems, Inc. 6–49. Courtesy of Lowenstein Inc. 6–50. Courtesy of Lux Steel Contract. 6–51. Courtesy of Lux Steel Contract. 6–52. Courtesy of Lowentein Inc. 6–53. Courtesy of Royal Custom Designs, Inc. 6–54.From *Interior Finish Materials for Health Care Facilities,* 1988. Courtesy of Charles C Thomas, Publisher, Springfield, Illinois. 6–55. Courtesy of Joerns Healthcare Inc. 6–56. Courtesy of Lowenstein Inc. 6–57. Courtesy of Royal Custom Designs, Inc. 6–58. Courtesy of Thonet Industries. 6–59. Courtesy of Joerns Healthcare Inc. 6–60. Courtesy of Thonet Industries. 6–61. Courtesy of Cy Mann Designs, Ltd. 6–62. Courtesy of The Charles Stewart Company. 6–63. Courtesy of Joerns Healthcare Inc. 6–64. Courtesy of Atelier International Ltd. 6–65. Courtesy of Cy Mann Designs, Ltd.

Chapter 7

7–1. Courtesy of NuTone Company. 7–2. Courtesy of Windmere. 7–3. Courtesy of Maxi-Aids: Illustration: Eric Weinburg. 7–4. Courtesy of Maxi-Aids: Illustration: Eric Weinburg. 7–5. Courtesy of Hammacher Schlemmer. 7–6. Courtesy of Maxi-Aids. 7–7. Courtesy of Egan Visual. 7–8. Courtesy of the Typewriting Institute for the Handicapped. 7–9. Courtesy of IBM National Support Center for Persons with Disabilities. 7–10. Courtesy of Human Factor Technologies Inc. 7–11. Courtesy of IBM National Support Center for Persons with Disabilities. 7–12. Reproduced with permission from American National Standard for Buildings and Facilities Providing Accessibility and Usability for Physically Handicapped People A117.1-1986, copyright 1986 by the American National Standards Institute. 7–13. Reproduced by permission from the 1984 Uniform Federal Accessibility Standards by the Publications Division, U.S. General Services Administration. 7–14. Courtesy of Ebco Manufacturing Co. 7–15. Reproduced by permission from the Americans With Disabilities Accessibility Guidelines, copyright 1991. 7–16. Reproduced by permission from the 1984 Uniform Federal Accessibility Standards by the Publications Division, U.S. General Services Administration. 7–17. Reprinted with permission of AT&T. 7–18. Reprinted with permission of AT&T. 7–19. Courtesy of Zygo Industries. 7–20. Courtesy of Southwestern Bell. 7–21. Courtesy of Mark Atkinson and Donna Cohn. 7–22. Courtesy of Hammacher Schlemmer. 7–23. Reprinted with permission of AT&T. 7–24. Reprinted with permission of AT&T. 7–25. Reprinted with permission of AT&T. 7–26. Reprinted with permission of AT&T. 7–27. Courtesy of Fleetwood. 7–28. Reprinted by permission from Wolfgang F. E. Preiser, Jacqueline C. Vischer, and Edward T. White, Designing Intervention, New York: Van Nostrand Reinhold, copyright 1991. 7–29. Courtesy of Garcia Imports. 7–30. Reproduced with permission from American National Standard for Buildings and Facilities Providing Accessibility and Usability for Physically Handicapped People A117.1-1986, copyright 1986 by the American National Standards Institute. 7–31. Courtesy of Apco. 7–32. Courtesy of Jan Roy. 7–33. Courtesy of Hammacher Schlemmer. 7–34. Courtesy of Casella Lighting. special order. 7–35. Courtesy of Casella Lighting. 7–36. Courtesy of Casella Lighting. 7–37. Courtesy of Clairson International. 7–38. Courtesy of Clairson International. 7–39. Courtesy Maxi-Aids. 7–40. Reproduced by permission of J.C. Penney Company, Inc. 1991.

Chapter 8

8–1. Photo courtesy of Whirlpool Corporation. 8–2. Courtesy of King Refrigeration Corp. 8–3. Reproduced by permission from Barrier Free Environments, Inc. for the U.S. Department of Housing and Urban Development Office of Policy Development and Research. 8–4. Reproduced with permission from American National Standard for Buildings and Facilities Providing Accessibility and Usability for Physically Handicapped People A117.1-1986, copyright 1986 by the American National Standards Institute. 8–5. Courtesy of Auton Company. 8–6. Courtesy of John Boos & Co. 8–7. Courtesy of Tielsa. 8–8. Courtesy of George A. Moore and Company.

8–9. Courtesy of Rev a Shelf Inc.   **8–10.** Courtesy of Clairson International. **8–11.** Courtesy of Lee/Rowan Company.   **8–12.** Courtesy of Hafele America Co. **8–13.** Courtesy of Hafele America Co.   **8–14.** Courtesy of Bertch Cabinet Manufacturing.   **8–15.** Courtesy of Hafele America Co.   **8–16.** Courtesy of Clairson International.   **8–17.** Reprinted by permission from S. C. Reznikoff, Interior Graphic and Design Standards. New York: Whitney Library of Design.   **8–18.** Courtesy of Hafele America Co.   **8–19.** Courtesy of Julius Blum Inc.   **8–20.** Courtesy of Julius Blum Inc.   **8–21.** Courtesy of Tielsa.   **8–22.** Courtesy of Constantine. **8–23.** Courtesy of The Ironmonger Inc.   **8–24.** Courtesy of Clairson International. **8–25.** Courtesy of Lifespec Cabinet Systems Inc.   **8–26.** Reproduced with permission from American National Standard for Buildings and Facilities Providing Accessibility and Usability for Physically Handicapped People A117.1-1986, copyright 1986 by the American National Standards Institute.   **8–27.** Photo courtesy of Whirlpool Corporation.   **8–28.** Reproduced by permission from Barrier Free Environments, Inc. for the U.S. Department of Housing and Urban Development Office of Policy Development and Research.   **8–29.** Reproduced by permission from the 1984 Uniform Federal Accessibility Standards by the Publications Division, U.S. General Services Administration.   **8–30.** Courtesy of Granberg Superior Systems Inc. **8–31.** Courtesy of Avonite, Inc.   **8–32.** Courtesy of Nevamar Corporation. **8–33.** Courtesy of Lifespec Cabinet Systems Inc.   **8–34.** Courtesy of Nevamar. **8–35.** Courtesy of Tielsa.   **8–36.** Courtesy of Whirlpool Corporation.   **8–37.** Courtesy of Whirlpool Corporation.   **8–38.** Photo courtesy of Bel-Art Products. **8–39.** Photo courtesy of Whirlpool Corporation.   **8–40.** Courtesy of NuTone Company.   **8–41.** Reproduced with permission of the copyright owner, General Electric Company.   **8–42.** Courtesy of Water Faucets.   **8–43.** Courtesy of Moen, Inc. **8–44.** Courtesy of Hastings Tile and Il Bagno Collection.   **8–45.** Courtesy of CN-Borma A.S.   **8–46.** Courtesy of Geberit Manufacturing, Inc.   **8–47.** Courtesy of Kindred Industries.   **8–48.** Courtesy of Abbaka.   **8–49.** Courtesy of George A. Moore and Company.   **8–50.** Reproduced by permission from Barrier Free Environments, Inc. for the U.S. Department of Housing and Urban Development Office of Policy Development and Research.   **8–51.** Reproduced by permission from Barrier Free Environments, Inc. for the U.S. Department of Housing and Urban Development Office of Policy Development and Research.   **8–52.** Courtesy of Gaggenau USA Corporation.   **8–53.** Reproduced with permission from American National Standard for Buildings and Facilities Providing Accessibility and Usability for Physically Handicapped People A117.1-1986, copyright 1986 by the American National Standards Institute.   **8–54.** Courtesy of DACOR.   **8–55.** Courtesy of DACOR.   **8–56.** Courtesy of Jenn Air Company.   **8–57.** Courtesy of Sub Zero Freezer Company, Inc. **8–58.** Courtesy of Penguin Products.   **8–59.** Photo courtesy of Whirlpool Corporation.   **8–60.** Photo courtesy of Whirlpool Corporation.   **8–61.** Photo courtesy of Whirlpool Corporation.   **8–62.** Reproduced by permission from Barrier Free Environments, Inc. for the U.S. Department of Housing and Urban Development Office of Policy Development and Research.   **8–63.** Courtesy of In-Sink Erator. **8–64.** Courtesy of Whirlpool.   **8–65.** Courtesy of Maxi-Aids.   **8–66.** Courtesy of Maxi-Aids.   **8–67.** Enrichments,® © 1991 Bissell Healthcare Corporation. **8–68.** Courtesy of Tielsa.   **8–69.** Courtesy of Bel-Art Products.   **8–70.** Courtesy of Bel-Art Products.   **8–71.** Enrichments,® © 1991 Bissell Healthcare Corporation.   **8–72.** Courtesy of Bel-Art Products.

Chapter 9

9–1. Reproduced by permission from Barrier Free Environments, Inc. for the U.S. Department of Housing and Urban Development Office of Policy Development and Research.   **9–2.** Courtesy of Health Resources Development, Inc. patented. **9–3.** Courtesy of TCT Company, Oberon Products. Photography: Barry Productions. **9–4.** Courtesy of Susan Behar ASID, Universal Design. Photography: Dan Forer. **9–5.** Reproduced with permission from American National Standard for Buildings and Facilities Providing Accessibility and Usability for Physically Handicapped People A117.1-1986, copyright 1986 by the American National Standards Institute.

9–6. Reproduced with permission from American National Standard for Buildings and Facilities Providing Accessibility and Usability for Physically Handicapped People A117.1-1986, copyright 1986 by the American National Standards Institute.   **9–7.** Courtesy of Kohler Co.   **9–8.** Courtesy of Kohler Co.   **9–9.** Reproduced by permission from Barrier Free Environments, Inc. for the U.S. Department of Housing and Urban Development Office of Policy Development and Research.   **9–10.** Courtesy of Watercolors Inc.   **9–11.** Courtesy of Memry Plumbing Products.   **9–12.** Courtesy of John F. Norris & Company, Inc., Symmons Industries.   **9–13.** Courtesy of Gemini Bath & Kitchen Products.   **9–14.** Reproduced with permission from American National Standard for Buildings and Facilities Providing Accessibility and Usability for Physically Handicapped People A117.1-1986, copyright 1986 by the American National Standards Institute.   **9–15.** Imported exclusively from Germany by Santile International Corporation.   **9–16.** Courtesy of NuTone Company. **9–17.** Reproduced with permission from American National Standard for Buildings and Facilities Providing Accessibility and Usability for Physically Handicapped People A117.1-1986, copyright 1986 by the American National Standards Institute.   **9–18.** Courtesy of American Standard.   **9–19.** Courtesy of Kohler Co.   **9–20.** Courtesy of the Silcraft Corporation.   **9–21.** Courtesy of Susan Behar ASID, Universal Design. Photography: Dan Forer.   **9–22.** Imported from Germany exclusively by Santile International Corporation, Houston, Texas.   **9–23.** Courtesy of Barrier Free Environments.   **9–24.** Courtesy of Kohler Co.   **9–25.** Courtesy of Cynthia Leibrock MA, ASID, Easy Access, Barrier Free Design Consultants. Illustration: Susan Behar ASID, Universal Design.   **9–26.** Courtesy of Susan Behar ASID, Universal Design. Photography: Dan Forer.   **9–27.** Courtesy of Susan Behar ASID, Universal Design. Photography: George Cott.   **9–28.** Courtesy of Kohler Co.   **9–29.** Reproduced with permission from American National Standard for Buildings and Facilities Providing Accessibility and Usability for Physically Handicapped People A117.1-1986, copyright 1986 by the American National Standards Institute.   **9–30.** Courtesy of Kohler Co.   **9–31.** Courtesy of Eljer Plumbingware.   **9–32.** Courtesy of Kohler Co.   **9–33.** Courtesy of Susan Behar ASID, Universal Design. Photography: Vernon Photography.   **9–34.** Courtesy of Kohler Co.   **9–35.** Courtesy of Healthguard.   **9–36.** Courtesy of NuTone Company.   **9–37.** Courtesy of Hastings Tile and Il Bagno Collection.   **9–38.** Reproduced by permission from the Americans With Disabilities Accessibility Guidelines, copyright 1991.   **9–39.** Courtesy of Villeroy & Boch USA Inc.   **9–40.** Courtesy of Dal-Tile.   **9–41.** Courtesy of Delta Faucet Company.   **9–42.** Courtesy of Kohler Co.   **9–43.** Courtesy of Delta Faucet Company.   **9–44.** Courtesy of Susan Behar ASID, Universal Design. Photography: Dan Forer.   **9–45.** Courtesy of Rutt Custom Cabinetry, Goodville, Pa. **9–46.** Courtesy of Susan Behar ASID, Universal Design. Photography: Dan Forer. **9–47.** Reprinted by permission from Barrier Free Environments.   **9–48.** Courtesy of Sunrise Medical Guardian.   **9–49.** Courtesy of HEWI.   **9–50.** Reproduced with permission from American National Standard for Buildings and Facilities Providing Accessibility and Usability for Physically Handicapped People A117.1-1986, copyright 1986 by the American National Standards Institute.   **9–51.** Reproduced with permission from American National Standard for Buildings and Facilities Providing Accessibility and Usability for Physically Handicapped People A117.1-1986, copyright 1986 by the American National Standards Institute.   **9–52.** Courtesy of HEWI.   **9–53.** Reproduced with permission from American National Standard for Buildings and Facilities Providing Accessibility and Usability for Physically Handicapped People A117.1-1986, copyright 1986 by the American National Standards Institute.   **9–54.** Courtesy of HEWI.   **9–55.** Courtesy of Bobrick Washroom Equipment, Inc. **9–56.** Courtesy of HEWI.   **9–57.** Courtesy of Iron-a-Way, Inc.   **9–58.** Courtesy of Miele Appliances Inc.

Appendices

AI–1, Courtesy of Susan Behar ASID, Universal Design. Illustration: Morton Plant Family Care, Clearwater, Fla.   **AII–1 and 2,** Courtesy of NAHB, National Research Center. Illustration: Adaptable Fire Safe House.

Copies of the *ANSI A117.1*-1986 may be purchased from the American National Standards Institute at 11 West 42nd Street, New York, NY 10036.

Copies of the 1984 *UFAS* may be purchased from the Publication Division, United States General Services Administration, GS Building, 18th and F Streets, NW, Washington, DC 20405.

Copies of *Adaptable Housing* may be purchased from Barrier Free Environments, Inc., Raleigh, NC 27622-0634.

Copies of *ADAAG* are available free of charge by calling 1-800-872-2252.

Index of Manufacturers

Abbaka
435—23 Street
San Francisco, CA 94107

Able Office
Georgia Institute of Technology
Atlanta, GA 30332-0130

Add Interior Systems Inc.
6500 South Avalon Boulevard
Los Angeles, CA 90003

Aiphone
P.O. Box 90075
Bellevue, WA 98009

Allsteel Phone/Data Products, Inc.
Allsteel Drive
Aurora, IL 60507-0871

American Lantern
4344 Highway 67 North
Newport, AR 72112

American Olean Tile Co.
1000 Cannon Avenue
Lansdale, PA 19446-0271

American Stair-Glide Corp.
4001 East 138 Street
Grandview, MO 64030

American Standard
Centennial Plaza
P.O. Box 6820
Piscataway, NJ 08855

Andersen Windows, Inc.
100 Fourth Avenue
Bayport, MN 55003-1096

Apco
388 Grant Street SE
Dept. S88
Atlanta, GA 30312-2227

Aquarius by Briggs
4350 West Cypress Street
Suite 800
Tampa, FL 33607

Artemide Company
1980 New Highway
Farmingdale, NY 11735

AT&T
131 Morristown Road
Basking Ridge, NJ 07920-1650

Atelier International, Ltd.
30-20 Thomson Avenue
Long Island City, NY 11101

Atlanta Thermoplastic Products
5032 N. Royal Atlanta Dr.
Tucker, GA 30084

Auton Co.
Box 1129
Sun Valley, CA 91353-1129

Avonite, Inc.
1945 Highway 3044
Belen, NM 87002

Baker Drapery Corp.
1116 West Pioneer Parkway
Peoria, IL 61615

Banner Scapes
7106 Mapleridge
Houston, TX 77081

Barrisol North America, Inc.
1340 Depot Street
Suite 110
Cleveland, OH 44116

Bel-Art Products
Maddock, Inc.
6 Industrial Road
Pequannock, NJ 07440-1993

Ben Grafton Ltd
145 Northwest 36
Miami, FL 33127

Benjamin Moore and Co.
51 Chestnut Ridge Road
Montvale, NJ 07645

Bertch Cabinet Mfg.
13-151 Merchandise Mart
Chicago, IL 60654

Bissell Healthcare Corp.
P.O. Box 3697
Grand Rapids, MI 49501-3697

Bobrick Washroom Equipment, Inc.
11611 Hart Street
North Hollywood, CA 91605

Bonar and Flotex, Inc.
8150 Springwood Drive
Suite 100
Irving, TX 75063

Casella Lighting
111 Rhode Island Street
San Francisco, CA 94103

The Charles Stewart Company
P.O. Box 5400
Hickory, SC 28603

Cheney
2445 South Calhoun Road
P.O. Box 51188
New Berlin, WI 53151

Clairson International
720 SW 17 Street
Ocala, FL 32674

CN-Borma A.S.
H. Guldbergsgade 14
DK-8700 Horsens
Denmark

Collins and Aikman Corp.
Floor Covering Division
311 Smith Industrial Boulevard
Dalton, GA 30722-1447

Conrad Imports, Inc.
575 Tenth Street
San Francisco, CA 94103-4884

Constantine
2050 Eastchester Road
Bronx, NY 10461

Construction Specialties, Inc.
P.O. Box 380
Route 405
Muncy, PA 17756

Custom Laminations, Inc.
932 Market Street
Paterson, NJ 07509-2066

Cy Mann Designs, Ltd.
979 Third Avenue
New York, NY 10022

DACOR
950 South Raymond Avenue
Pasadena, CA 91109

Dal-Tile
1135 Reed Hartman Highway
Cincinnati, OH 45241

Delta Faucet Co.
P.O. Box 40980
Indianapolis, IN 46280

Dimango Products
7528 Kensington Road
Brighton, MI 48116

Duro-Med Industries, Inc.
138 Kansas Street
Hackensack, NJ 07602

Durotest Corp
9 Law Drive
Fairfield, NJ 07007

Ebco Manufacturing Company
265 North Hamilton Road
P.O. Box 1315
Columbus, OH 43213-0150

Egan Visual
6085 Rickenbacker Road
Commerce, CA 90040

Eljer Plumbingware
901 Tenth Street
Plano, TX 85086-9037

Ello Furniture Manufacturing Co.
1350 Preston Street
Rockford, IL 61102

Enrichments
Bissell Healthcare Corp.
P.O. Box 579
Hinsdale, IL 60521

Eurotex Inc.
165 West Ontario Street
Philadelphia, PA 19140

Fleetwood
P.O. Box 1259
Holland, MI 49422-1259

Gaggenau USA Corp.
425 University Avenue
Norwood, MA 02062

Garcia Imports
P.O. Box 5066
Redwood City, CA 94063

Gemini Bath and Kitchen Products
3790 East 44 Street
Suite 228
Tucson, AZ 85713

General Electric Co.
Building 4, Appl. Park
Louisville, KY 40225

George A. Moore and Co. Ltd.
Thorp Arch Trading Estate
Wetherby, West Yorkshire
LS237DD England

Gerberit Manufacturing, Inc.
1100 Boone Drive
Michigan City, IN 46360

Grandberg Superior Systems
2502 Thayer Avenue
Saskatoon, Saskatchewan,
Canada 57L 5Y2

Hafele America Co.
3901 Cheyenne Drive
Archdale, NC 27263

Halo Lighting
400 Busse Road
Elk Grove Village, IL 60007

Hammacher Schlemmer
P.O. Box 7913
Mount Prospect, IL 60056-7913

The Harbinger Co., Inc.
P.O. Box 1209
Calhoun, GA 30701

Hastings Tile and Il Bagno
Collection
30 Commercial Street
Freeport, NY 11520

Haworth Inc.
One Haworth Center
Holland, MI 49423-9576

Healthguard
P.O. Box 60113
Chicago, IL 60660

Health Resources Development,
Inc.
6112 East Mockingbird Lane
Paradise Valley, AZ 85253

HEWI
2851 Old Tree Drive
Lancaster, PA 17603

Honeywell
1985 Douglas Drive N.
Golden Valley, MN 55422-3992

Howe Furniture Corp.
12 Cambridge Drive
Trumbull, CT 06611

Human Factor Technologies, Inc.
55 Harvey Road
Londonderry, NH 03053

IBM Nat'l Support Center for
Persons with Disabilities
P.O. Box 2150
Atlanta, GA 30301

Industrial Fabrics Assoc. Int'l
345 Cedar Building
Suite 800
St. Paul, MN 55101

In-Sink Erator
Emerson Electric
4700 21 Street
Racine, WI 53406-5093

Innovations in Wallcoverings
22 W 21 St
New York, NY 10010

Iron-A-Way, Inc.
220 West Jackson
Morton, IL 61550

The Ironmonger, Inc.
1822 West Sheffield Avenue
Chicago, IL 60614

J.C. Penney Co., Inc.
Circulation Department
Box 2056
Milwaukee, WI 53201-2056

Jenn Air Company
3035 Shadeland
Indianapolis, IN 46226-0901

Joanna Western Mills
1 Park Ave
New York, NY 10016

Joerns Healthcare, Inc.
Joerns Sunrise Medical
5555 Joerns Drive
Stevens Point, WI 54481-0208

John Boos & Co.
315 South First
Effingham, IL 62401

John R. Norris Company, Inc.
42 Thomas Patten Drive
Randolph, MA 02368

Julius Blum, Inc.
Blum Ind. Park
Highway 16—Lowesvile
Stanley, NC 28164

Kimball Healthcare Co.
1600 Royal Street
Jasper, IN 47549

Kimball Hospitality Furniture, Inc.
2602 North Newton Street
Jasper, IN 47549

Kindred Industries
1000 Kindred Road
P.O. Box 190
Midland, Ontario, Canada L4R 4K9

King Refrigeration Corp.
76-02 Woodhaven Boulevard
Glendale, NY 11385

The Knoll Group
655 Madison Avenue
New York, NY 10021

Kohler Co.
Highland Drive
Kohler, WI 53044

Lee/Rowan Co.
6333 Etzel Avenue
St. Louis, MO 63133

Leviton Manufacturing Co., Inc.
59-25 Little Neck Parkway
Little Neck, NY 11362

Lifespec Cabinet Systems, Inc.
428 North Lamar Boulevard
Oxford, MS 38655

Lightworks
3345 West Hunting Park Avenue
Philadelphia, PA 19132

Ligne Roset USA
200 Lexington Avenue
New York, NY 10016

LouverDrape
1100 Colorado Avenue
Santa Monica, CA 90401

Lowenstein Inc.
P.O. Box 10369
Pompano Beach, FL 33061-6369

Lumex, Inc.
100 Spence Street
Bayshore, NY 11706

Lutron Electronics Co., Inc.
205 Suter Road
Coopersburg, PA 18036

Lux Steel Contract
2135 Industrial Parkway
Elkhart, IN 46516

Mastervoice
10523 Humbolt Street
Los Alamitos, CA 90720

Maxi Aids, Inc.
42 Executive Boulevard
P.O. Box 3209
Farmindale, NY 11735

McGuire and Company
1201 Bryant Avenue
San Francisco, CA 94103

Memry Pumbing Products
P.O. Box 548
Worcester, MA 01613

Mercer Products, Inc.
4455 Dardanelle Drive
Orlando, FL 32808

Metropolitan Furniture Corp.
245 East Harris Avenue
San Francisco, CA 94080-6807

Miele Appliances, Inc.
22D Worlds Fair Drive
Somerset, NJ 08873

Milcor/Lima Register
P.O. Box 28
Lima, OH 45002-0028

Moen, Inc.
377 Woodland Avenue
Elyria, OH 44036

Monsanto Chemical Co.
320 Interstate North Parkway
Atlanta, GA 30339

National Products, Inc.
912 Baxter Avenue
Louisville, KY 40204

Nevamar Corporation.
8339 Telegraph Road
Odenton, MD 21113

NOVA Technologies, Inc.
39 Cabot Court
Unit L
Hauppauge, NY 11788

NuTone Company
Madison and Red Bank Roads
Cincinnati, OH 45227-1599

The Pace Collection Inc.
351 Peachtree Hills Avenue NE
Atlanta, GA 30305

Palazzetti, Inc.
515 Madison Avenue
New York, NY 10022

Pella Windows
102 Main Street
Pella, Iowa 50219

Penquin Products
47 NE 11 Way
Deerfield Beach, FL 33441

PermaGrain Products, Inc.
13 West Third Street
Media, PA 19063

Pinecrest
2118 Blaisdell Avenue
Minneapolis, MN 55404

Presso-Matic
3048 Industrial 33 Street
Fort Pierce, FL 34946-8694

Rain Bird Sales, Inc.
Commercial Division
145 North Grand Avenue
Glendora, CA 91740

Research Products Corp.
P.O. Box 1467
Madison, WI 53701-1467

Rev A Shelf, Inc.
2409 Plantside Drive
Jeffersontown, KY 40299

Roppe
1602 N Union St
Box X
Fostoria, OH 44830

Royal Custom Designs, Inc.
1449 Industrial Park Street
Covina, CA 91722

Rutt Custom Cabinetry
1564 Main Street
P.O. Box 129
Goodville, PA 17528

Samson McCann Furniture
638 Ramona Street
Palo Alto, CA 94301

Santile International Corp.
1201 West Loop North
Suite 170
Houston, TX 77055

Shaw Industries, Inc.
P.O. Drawer 2128
Dalton, GA 30722-2128

Sico Incorporated
7525 Cahill Road
P.O. Box 1169
Minneapolis, MN 55440

The Silcraft Corp.
528 Hughes Drive
Traverse City, MI 49684

Silent Gliss USA Inc.
P.O. Box 405
Loganville, GA 30249

Sonic Alert Systems
1750 West Hamlin Road
Rochester Hille, MI 48309

Southwestern Bell
1000 Des Peres Road
St. Louis, MO 63131

Spanjier Bros., Inc.
1160 North House Street
Chicago, IL 60610-2490

Spectus Systems
1301 Garfield Avenue
Superior, WI 54880

Stanley Magic-Door
Route 6 & Hyde Road
Farmington, CT 06032

Sub Zero Freezer Co. Inc.
P.O. Box 4130
Madison, WI 53711

Sunrise Medical Guardian
Guardian Products, Inc.
12800 Wentworth Street
Box C-4522
Arletta, CA 91331-4522

Tempo Industries
2002 A South Grand Avenue
Santa Ana, CA 92705

Thonet Industries
403 Mecham Road
P.O. Box 5900
Statesville, NC 28677

Tielsa
Postfach 3620
Industriestrabe 14-18
D-4902 Bad Salzuflen
Germany

TCT Products, Oberon Products
4260 Kearney Street
Denver, CO 80216

Typewriting Inst. for the
Handicapped
3102 West Augusta Avenue
Phoenix, AZ 85051

Unity Systems, Inc.
2606 Spring Street
Redwood City, CA 94063

USG Interiors, Inc.
101 South Wacker Drive
Chicago, IL 60606-4385

Vecta Contract
1800 South Great SW Parkway
Grand Prairie, TX 75053

Villeroy and Boch USA Inc.
Interstate 80 at New Maple
Avenue
Pinebrook, NJ 07068

Watercolors, Inc.
Garrison on Hudson
New York, NY 10524

Water Facets
3001 Redhill Building
Costa Mesa, CA 92626

Wesley Allen, Inc.
1001 East 60 Street
Los Angeles, CA 90001

Whirlpool Corp.
2000 M-63
Benton Harbor, MI 49022-2692

Windmere Products
Miami Lakes, FL 33014

Winona Industries, Inc.
602 East Front Street
Winona, MN 55987

Workstations, Inc.
165 Front Street
Chicopee, MA 01013

York Spiral Stair
Route 32
North Vassalboro, ME 04962

Zygo Industries, Inc.
Post Office Box 1008
Portland, OR 97207-1008

For additional manufacturers or replacements for specific products, a computer search can be conducted by:

Marian Hall
NEWINGTON CHILDREN'S HOSPITAL
181 E. Cedar St.
Newington, CT 06111
203 667-5405

or

The Institute for Technology Development
Advanced Living Systems Division
428 North Lamar Blvd.
Oxford, MS 38655-3204
601 234-0158

Index